A CAREGIVER'S DAILY COMPANION

by Undine Brereton

A Caregiver's Daily Companion
Trilogy Christian Publishers A Wholly Owned Subsidiary of Trinity Broadcasting Network
2442 Michelle Drive, Tustin, CA 92780

For information about special discounts for bulk purchases, please contact Trilogy Christian Publishing.

Manufactured in the United States of America
10 9 8 7 6 5 4 3 2 1
Library of Congress Cataloging-in-Publication Data is available.
ISBN: 979-8-88738-206-7
E-ISBN: 979-8-88738-207-4

Dedication

Dedicated to someone special in my life. She is stronger than she thinks, my daughter, Afiya Clarke.

Acknowledgment

Thank you to everyone in my life who inspires me to always do better. Every word written is true; some names may be changed in order to protect the identity of individuals.

Dec 2023

My brother Chuck
May God continue to
bless and keep u in
Jesus name!

author: [illegible] B.

Table of Contents

Preface 9

Janet 13

Nurse Anka 55

Amiga 79

Ms. Monica 103

Meme 187

Gabriel 275

About the Author 373

Closing Note. 375

Preface

The year 2020 began like every other year. Amidst the New Year, with Christmas bills to pay, there was disturbing news on the horizon. It was about the epidemic that was transpiring in China. At that time, China seemed so far away, and the news was just that, news. It was not until one day in February, after coming home violently sick from work, that my view of this news of the virus began to change. I left work that day at 6:00 p.m. and got home around 7:00 p.m. By the time I got home, I felt every bone in my body hurting; my throat and head felt like they were about to split. I had a roasting fever, my mouth tasted bitter, and I could not smell anything. Another interesting development was that my stomach felt terrible, and it was challenging to walk.

When I entered my home that night, I just dropped all my bags on the floor at the front door. I dragged myself upstairs and lay on the bed, fully dressed. My husband, so caring and concerned, quickly came upstairs with a cup of hot tea, but I didn't have the energy to drink it. I just lay there moaning and groaning, clutching my stomach. With these symptoms coupled with symptoms of menopause, like hot flashes, I really believed that I was on my way to meet Jesus. I eventually fell asleep, and later at some point, I remember looking at the clock and seeing that it was a little after 4:00 a.m. I then got my phone out of my pocket and compiled a text message to my employers, letting them know I was not coming in to work that day because I was unwell and did not want to expose them to what I had contracted.

I was determined that whatever was attacking me had to go in Jesus' name. My prayers were heard by God and answered. With a few failed attempts, I eventually managed to sit up that morning. With my head and body hurting, I began to walk around, all the while praying, and I cried out to God. Going down the stairs was difficult; I was soaked in my own perspiration. However, I persisted, no more lying in bed. By Monday, I was back out to work; still, news from China was coming in. By the beginning of March, America began announcing many cases of the deadly virus called COVID-19.

By March 17th, 2020, I was on my final day of work in New York City. All states declared a state of emergency. Humans were dying daily by the thousands. I lost so many friends to the grip of the virus; death was everywhere. But at the center of it all, I believed that God was always there.

I had failed to successfully acquire unemployment benefits, but eventually, after many attempts, I was granted unemployment benefits. Fortunately, I was blessed with a job not long after with Amazon, which is five minutes away from my home.

I would like to mention that COVID-19, amongst other things, drew me closer to God. I was studying God's Word more and encouraging others not to give up. I know everyone was affected by the pandemic, but there is a group of people who felt pressured but were true unsung heroes in all of it. The people I am referring to are the caregivers in every capacity. Whether they were doctors, nurses, medics, ambulance drivers, cleaners, parents, teachers, siblings, aunts, uncles, grandparents, nannies, governesses, baby nurses, service officers, garbage collectors, and you, if you were not mentioned, you were a hero also, as you gave care in some capacity. I wanted to give my support by writing a prayer from Monday to Friday and sending them on those mornings to encourage my fellow caregivers. I started writing short prayers, but they grew lengthy as time went by. Many days I would be moved to tears. I felt like God was literally writing for me. I pray that this book will encourage someone in their life's journey. This is a compilation of daily encouragement to all caregivers.

In the initial stages, my writings were simple and extremely short, as you will see for yourselves. I did not know the impact it truly was making on the people I shared them with. Furthermore, I did not believe it had much of an impact at first because my aim was simply to encourage anyone with my words and to lead one person to Christ.

Now I see that God has given me a gift. A gift I want to share in this book. Yet with my simple words, He elevated them not only to touch and uplift the hearts of others downtrodden and in despair but also to bring them to the point of spiritual change, closer to Christ.

I am grateful to God for blessing these hands to write, and with my words, I hope to continue letting the light of the Almighty God illuminate the lives of all those who choose to read this little book of prayer and encouragement.

Janet

Janet migrated to the United States of America about twenty-five years ago from Trinidad and Tobago. After a failed abusive marriage and fearing for her life, she sadly fled, leaving behind three small children. Her plan was to be able to one day soon bring them to America also. She later on learned firsthand that mankind makes plans, but God has a much better and bigger one. Migrating to America on a visitor visa is one thing, but getting permanent residency is another. They are referred to as "illegal immigrants," cleaning people's homes and taking care of their children were some of the jobs that were available. One thing observed is that many born and bred Americans have no heart when seeking to replace their responsibilities by hiring someone who is "illegal." They may pay them little or nothing, with no benefits or insurance, to work and be treated inhumanely. These persons who are waiting and hiding in the shadows tolerate the abuse with hopes that one day things will get better.

Janet fell into that category of being an "illegal immigrant." But to make things even more difficult, she began to look for love in all the wrong places, which many times caused her more pain. Her first love was Fred from Grenada, who was living with another woman, his wife at the time. Fred's wife was working as a live-in help on Long Island. So Janet began visiting Fred and warming his bed while his wife was away. It ended when Janet got pregnant and had a painful abortion. She soon after picked up Ron, who was a drug pusher. He committed murder and went to jail for life. Janet was left with two children by Ron to raise. While scrambling to raise these two children by herself, she had to put one child in daycare and take one with her to work.

Janet's job was with a family that had three children, all under the age of five, and hers made it four. Janet's job as a caregiver wore many hats on a daily basis. She was a doctor, chef, mother, grandparent, seamstress, technician, nurse, housekeeper, accountant, errand person, and the list continues. I would jokingly refer to her as a Domestic Engineer who graduated from the university of "Hard Knocks and Dirty Socks." Janet overworked herself to the point where when she got home, she was too tired to properly take care of her own children. Her patience was thin, always wondering when things would get better for her.

It is people like Janet that inspired me to write each day a word of encouragement. During the pandemic, she was unable to work because her job could not be done virtually. She was not legally recognized, so unemployment relief was not possible. She eventually lost her apartment, and her two children died from COVID-19. In 2021, she told me what kept her going was my daily motivational pieces I shared with her. It motivated me so much knowing that she felt encouraged by my writings that I decided to write this book so others can be encouraged as well. I learned many things during the pandemic, but one thing that stood out the most was that when you trust God with your heart, He blesses you in the overflow. These are the actual daily encouragement as I wrote them in March 2020. Read them during your daily Bible devotions, and on the lines below, write a response to encourage yourself positively throughout the day. May you be blessed by these words.

1

Many blessings to all caregivers!

"This is the day the LORD has made; we will rejoice…" (Psalm 118:24, KJV)

For some, the day may seem rough, but let's not forget that it's up to God and then us to make our day good. I do agree that everyone's circumstance at their job site is different. I will explain how I approach the day, and by God's grace, it will always go well. I approach my day by praying and Thanksgiving to God first. Asking for wisdom in each encounter during my day. I also believe in making declarations over my life, my family, my friends, the leaders, and the government of nations. Studying God's Word is very important; reading your Bible daily is a must. When you put your hands in the hands of our Father and our LORD Jesus Christ the devil is going to flee from you.

Have a beautiful day in Jesus' name, amen. Shalom!

____

____

____

____

____

____

2

Today's prayer!

Lord Jesus,

I lift up every caregiver before You. May You grant them more patience, courage, and endurance. The job that they perform daily is very challenging at times, but let them all be prayerful and watchful. Miracles are happening right now in our lives. May their employers be always generous and kind and pour out financial blessings because they deserve it, in Jesus' name.

In Esther 4:13–14, Mordecai admonished Esther to stand up for her people and to intercede on their behalf. Let's stand up for each other; let's pray for each other. So that our day at work will be like a minute, and we would return to our home stress-free in Jesus' name. Let's keep the fire burning for Christ Jesus. That's where our strength comes from.

Stay blessed! Shalom!

____

____

____

____

____

____

3

Hello, caregivers!

This morning, in the name of Jesus Christ, I send out these prayers to all caregivers in Christ. You are not alone; God, our Heavenly Father, is with you. Don't forget to thank God for all His blessings, mercies, and grace today and always. Let's keep the fire burning for Christ the triune God in Jesus' name, amen. The Lord is your strength, amen!

I pray in the name of Jesus this morning for courage, patience, wisdom, grace, and endurance as we maneuver our daily chores. I also encourage those who may be going through situations to be strong in the Lord. Jesus already paid the price, so let us live in the abundance of His Blessings, amen! Hallelujah! Keep the fire burning for God, and be diligent in reading your Bible every day.

Stay in peace, love, and happiness in Jesus' name. Shalom!

____

____

____

____

____

____

4

Question, caregivers!

Do all of you believe that Jesus Christ loves you? Blessed morning, caregivers. I greet you in the wonderful, mighty, marvelous name of our Lord and Savior, Jesus Christ. The answer to my question, I hope, is yes, amen! God sent His Son, Jesus, to Earth, in a human body, preaching and teaching the gospel, later giving his life on the cross at Calvary. It was for you and me. Hallelujah! He woke all of us up this morning because He loves us. Trust in God, believe in His *Word*, do what is right and from your heart, and serve Him in Spirit and in truth. When you trust God with your heart, He will trust you with the kingdom of heaven. Have a Blessed day in the mighty name of Jesus Christ. Shalom!

____

____

____

____

____

____

5

Gracious morning, caregivers!

Greetings in Jesus' name! It is the name above all names; there is power in the name of Jesus. When situations happen, shout out the name of Jesus! Jesus! Jesus!... Hallelujah! We are more than conquerors when we place absolutely *all* of our trust in Jesus. Keep God in your thoughts, meditate on Him day and night and watch miracles happen in our lives. Tremendous blessings in Jesus' name, amen.

Stay focused on God and hang on to the hem of His garment. Our jobs may be tedious at times, but by God's grace, we will continue to make it. Thank God for sending His Son, Jesus, to die for our sins. I feel happy today, knowing that all of my sins have been washed away by the blood of Jesus. Don't ever allow the devil to try his tricks with you; he is trying to steal your joy. We serve a God of love. This morning, Heavenly Father protected our loved ones and us. Please continue to pray for our governments and leaders throughout the world. Keep the fire burning for Jesus Christ in your hearts, amen, and amen! Shalom!

6

Oh, Happy day, caregivers!

God is worthy of all our praise, hallelujah! As we go through this day, Lord Jesus, we put You first. Hallelujah! Hallelujah! You are worthy, Lord! In the name of Jesus, take full control over every situation that the enemy may try to direct in our way today and reverse it, Lord! Today as we humble ourselves before You, Father, may our hearts be forever grateful and filled with gratitude as we approach our day with thanksgiving. Jesus' love is for all of us this morning. Don't harden your hearts, for tomorrow is not promised to you. Tell someone about Jesus today, hallelujah! And how He woke us up this morning. Let's keep the fire burning in our hearts for God, in Jesus' mighty name, amen. Shalom!

____

____

____

____

____

____

7

Good morning, caregivers!

I trust that your week was good and will continue to be good in Jesus' name. Amen! Saints of God, let us all reach out to each other in the upcoming week and encourage one another. Tell someone about Jesus and the price He paid for our transgressions. May your day be filled with peace, love, and happiness. Be safe today on your commute in Jesus' name. Never forget you are not alone. Our Father in heaven sees and knows everything. Stay strong, healthy, and wise, and be safe in Jesus Christ, amen. Shalom!

____

____

____

____

____

____

8

Blessed morning to all caregivers!

May the peace that passeth all understanding be with each of us today. Let's not forget who our God is, hallelujah! Caregivers, we serve a God who knows everything. He is the God of the universe, and His love is limitless. My prayer is for you to stay connected to God. Remember, "We can do all things through Christ who strengthens [us]" (Philippians 4:13, NKJV). (Hereinafter, brackets added for clarity.) In your darkest moment, remember God is always there. In the midst of sickness, death, hardship, and pain, our good, good Heavenly Father loves you.

Let us acknowledge our Heavenly Father today and always, hallelujah! Hallelujah! All lives matter to God. Let's prepare ourselves to meet the King of Glory, who is coming soon. *Berakah* (blessings) and peace in Jesus' name, amen. Shalom!

9

God's amazing grace, caregivers!

Blessings, blessings, and more blessings to all of you. Count your blessings today, list them below, and recount them throughout your day if you start forgetting the mercies of God:

____

____

____

____

____

____

We made it to another day; all praise belongs to God. It's not because we were good; it's because of God's mercies and grace towards us. Let us keep on thanking God as we go about this day. When we praise God, there is an atmospheric shift, and the impossible becomes possible. We serve a mighty, awesome, loving Alpha and Omega God. Let's keep on pressing on in prayers, and humble supplication, in Jesus' name, amen. Shalom!

10

Good morning, caregivers!

Be blessed in Jesus' name. Let's honor God, our Heavenly Father, today with praise and thanksgiving. Hallelujah to the King of Glory. Let's go before God with simple words, speaking from your heart; let Him know how much you love and trust Him, amen. Sometimes we may get too busy rushing around trying to get things done, but stop for a moment and remember to think about who woke all of us up this morning; it was the grace of God. The enemy wants to distract us from God but stay focused on Jesus Christ. Be encouraged today because we have a soul to save and a God to glorify, amen. Be encouraged today. God loves us all, and Jesus Christ is always Lord. Shalom! I implore you to write a prayer below and keep it in your hearts as you go along with your day.

____

____

____

____

____

____

11

Praise be to God this morning, for He is good,
and His mercies are everlasting!

Good morning, caregivers,

I greet you in the only true and living name of Jesus of Christ. Hallelujah! He is worthy of all of our praise, so let's take a moment to tell Him thanks for everything. The love between our Father and us is unending. It is satisfying and always more than enough. I trust that everyone who is reading these words solidifies in your heart that Jesus loves you. I pray tremendous blessings upon all of us today and always in Jesus' name.

In the many jobs that we all execute daily, which take patience, courage, strength, endurance, and love, may God's angels surround us, hallelujah. No matter what the enemy (the devil) may try, don't give in, and don't give up. God is always working on our behalf, even when we don't think so, amen. Be encouraged today, caregivers, trust God with all your heart, and He would trust you with heaven. Be strong in the Lord, our Savior, Jesus Christ, amen, amen, and amen. Shalom!

____

____

____

____

12

Blessings to all caregivers!

I pray that this day goes by quickly and stress-free in Jesus' name. Keep your eyes on Jesus, and all will be well with you, hallelujah. Jesus' love is everlasting. My morning encouragement is to give thanks unto God for waking us up this morning, hallelujah. As we go about our business today, may we find that peace and joy that exceeds all understanding in Jesus' Almighty name. Put all your trust in God today because we are loved by God, our Father. We give You, Lord, all the praise and honor in Jesus' name, amen. Let this year be of unlimited blessings in Jesus' name, amen. Shalom!

____

____

____

____

____

____

13

Blessed morning!

I bless all caregivers in the mighty name of Jesus Christ. Hallelujah! Hallelujah! We serve the only, true, living God. Let's give Him all the praise and honor today in the name of Jesus. As we maneuver throughout this day, I pray for courage, peace, love, grace, blessings, and patience in all that we do, in the name of Jesus.

In this field, patience is so hard to have; we get impatient with our situation, our employers, and with the duties we must complete. Our patience runs thin when we care for others, but never forget that caring and serving others selflessly is a gift that angels like us are blessed with daily. When it becomes overwhelming and your cup begins to overflow with regret and stress, ask God to tip your cup over into His so you can bear some more. We give you all the glory and praise in no other name but the name of Jesus Christ, amen. Shalom!

____

____

____

____

____

____

14

Greetings, caregivers, in the powerful name of Jesus Christ!

We're making it by God's grace. The battle is not ours; it belongs to our creator Jesus Christ. Let's not carry around on our shoulders unnecessary baggage today. Hallelujah! If your job is tough, put it to God, and He will make it easier. Sometimes we try to fight up with the trials of life on our own. We have a friend in Jesus who is ever ready to bear all our sins and grief. Hallelujah! Hallelujah! Our Lord and Savior, Jesus Christ, already paid the price for our sins.

I declare and decree that each and every one of us under the blood of Jesus Christ is blessed in Jesus' name. I declare and decree that our family is blessed in Jesus' name. And that all of our heart's desires are granted in the mighty name of Jesus Christ, amen. Let's keep the fire in our hearts burning for the love of God, amen, amen. Have a truly healthy and happy weekend. What are some of your heart's desires, write them on paper and seal it in your hearts so that you never forget what you are aiming for in Jesus' name. Shalom!

___

___

___

___

15

Caregivers in Christ!

Let us put on the full armor of God. We are here on this Earth for a purpose, which is to take care of the Earth and everyone/thing in it. Let no man tell you, "You cannot do it," or "You are not capable." The Scripture says, "I can do all things through Christ who strengthens me" (Philippians 4:13, NKJV). Let us take our rightful place in this land of the living. I pray that we all receive these words in our hearts in Jesus' mighty name. Let us all give a loud praise to God our Father in heaven for His everlasting mercies and grace. Amen!

____

____

____

____

____

____

16

Pleasant good morning, caregivers!

Greetings in the mighty name of Jesus Christ. As the scripture so rightfully says, "This is the day which the LORD has made; we shall rejoice and be glad in it" (Psalm 118:24, KJV). Hallelujah! Regardless of how bad our situation is, we can choose to stay in the situation or get out of it, amen! When we trust in God, miracles happen. I am reaching out to those who may be reading this encouraging message today.

If you have not made Jesus Christ the center of your life, please do so before it's too late. Let's reach out and encourage one another today and share the love of Jesus Christ. Who do you know that is struggling today? What would you tell them if you had the chance? Do it today and bless someone. Hallelujah, hallelujah; we serve a God who is alive, hallelujah. Glory to God in the highest. Be blessed, in Jesus' name, amen. Shalom!

____

____

____

____

____

____

17

Blessings, caregivers!

The name of Jesus Christ is worthy to be praised always. I trust everyone is standing on the Word of truth, which is the scriptures of the Bible. Hallelujah, hallelujah! How quickly time is going by, let's prepare ourselves to meet the King of Glory. God is coming soon and sooner than we expect. Hallelujah! I want all of us to be in the number John the Baptist saw in his vision.

Take time and study the book of Revelation this morning. Our father has been taking good care of us and will continue to take care of us. That is why we have to honor Him with thanksgiving, with our praise. Don't be afraid to stand on God's Word. My message is quite simple: Serve God our Lord in spirit and in truth, and let Him lead your life, in Jesus' mighty name, amen. Shalom!

18

Good morning, caregivers!

I greet you in no other name but the name of Christ Jesus.

May the good Lord bless and keep us as we go through the day in Jesus' name. Let's open our mouths and thank God for another day, hallelujah! If it wasn't for the goodness of God, where would we be? We can either be part of the solution in Christ Jesus or be part of the problem with the enemy; the choice is always ours. We must always remember that our Heavenly Father Jesus Christ loves us. It's a love that no man can have or give to us. Trust God with all your hearts today, and He will trust you with the kingdom of heaven. Be a blessing today, in Jesus' name, amen. Shalom!

19

Pleasant day to all caregivers!

Ever asked yourself why is the time going by so quickly? The answer is in God's Word. Study Matthew 24:22–24 (KJV) and see why God is shortening the days and the spiritual benefits in Him doing so. My encouragement today is to let us prepare ourselves to meet the King, hallelujah, hallelujah; His name is Jesus Christ our Savior. Believers in Christ, let us all adore Him, let us trust Him with our whole hearts. Have a great weekend in Jesus' name, amen, amen. Shalom!

____

____

____

____

____

____

20

Blessed morning to all caregivers!

Greetings, in the mighty name of Jesus Christ. Are you happy to see another day? I am, but it's not because it is all going good; it's only because God is good. It is all in God's hands, everything we go through daily. Hallelujah, let us thank God for all His blessings and mercies. I pray over each of you today in the name of Jesus Christ. Hallelujah, God has been so good to me; I am overwhelmed by His love.

I want the world to know about the love affair between my God and me, and it's available to everyone who believes and trusts Him with everything. Be encouraged today; trust God with your family; trust Him with your marriage. He will make everything better. Trust God with children; He will protect them. Don't be troubled by the trials of life. God's got us. Have a wonderful, Happy day, in Jesus' name, amen, amen. Shalom! Who is praying for today?

____

____

____

____

____

____

21

Sweet blessings, caregivers!

Good morning, I greet you in the name of Jesus Christ, amen. I trust everyone is staying under the blood of Jesus Christ, hallelujah. Just relax and ride out the storm of life. Place all your faith in our Heavenly Father so that we may live in peace, love, and harmony with each. Do you remember the first day you immigrated to America? Did you think that your life would turn out this way? Did you think that you would struggle this much to provide for your family? Did you believe a caregiver is what you would have to resort to? What did you really think it would be like, and where do you see yourself? Write it below and pray on it; God is still working on your behalf, even while in your current position. Have a Blessed day, in Jesus' name, amen, Shalom!

____

____

____

____

____

____

22

A big shout-out to all caregivers!

I want you to know that there is power in the name of Jesus Christ. In everything that we do, let's keep the most powerful name on our lips; Jesus! Jesus! Jesus! Many blessings upon you, your family, your job, your health, and everything and everyone you come in contact with in Jesus' name. Hallelujah, our God is worthy to be praised, worthy to be glorified. Keep the faith, knowing that Jesus already paid the price. When God sent His Son, Jesus, to temporarily assume a human body and die on the cross, it was for us all. Hallelujah, it was for us to have that abundance of life.

Here is where we all should be saying, "Thank You, Lord, for shedding Your blood." All of our sins have been washed away; no more condemnation as written in John 3:16 (KJV). This is the best news; the price is already paid; hallelujah, hallelujah. We are new people in Christ. Let's live the royal way. Step with purpose, never doubting what God can do, amen. I pray that someone somewhere finds comfort knowing we have a father who sees and knows everything and loves us still. Keep trusting in God for your breakthrough, hallelujah, hallelujah. It's coming in Jesus' name, amen, and amen. Shalom!

23

Blessed morning, caregivers!

It's nice to know that we have a friend in Jesus. At the Calvary cross, He bears our sins and shame, so we may be set free. Not some, but all of our troubles we can take to God in prayer, hallelujah, hallelujah. God is everything, amen. Just accept and trust Him, for your miracles, for your breakthrough, for your healing, for your new and better job, for your marriage, for your children, for your salary increase, and for your Christian husband. Whatever it may be, just trust God. Jesus Christ is the beginner and finisher of everything. Be blessed in Jesus' name, amen. Shalom!

____

____

____

____

____

____

24

Good morning and blessings to all caregivers!

We are getting by the Grace of God, caregivers in Christ. We were created in the image and likeness of God, don't be afraid to utilize that power in the name of Jesus Christ. Hallelujah, hallelujah! I continue to pray that God grants us courage and strength to face the day, no matter what. Look at the rising of the sun this morning and be thankful for another day.

How many times have you taken for granted your blessing to be alive? Do you realize that each new day signifies mercy from God? We made mistakes yesterday; some of us even forgot to pray for forgiveness. We have sinned our worst sin and treated someone with scorn or disdain. Why, then, would God favor us with life today? It's only by His grace we are here, but not to squander this new chance. Have a wonderful weekend in Jesus' name, amen, amen. Shalom!

____

____

____

____

____

____

25

It is a new morning, caregivers!

Be encouraged in the name of Jesus Christ. I want to share the power of having and exercising your faith. I learned to trust in God for everything. I have seen and currently experiencing the blessings of faith-filled declarations over my life. I was lost in sin; Jesus Christ took care of all of my sins. Because we were born in sin, we are all sinners, but by the bloodshed on the Calvary cross, we were made clean.

Our Heavenly Father doesn't hold on to things we have done. We have to confess our sins before God, and they will be thrown into the sea of forgetfulness forever. Be encouraged today, whatever your situation may be or whatever you are trusting God to do. Don't give up. Hallelujah, trust in God and be of good courage; it will come through, amen. Go about your day believing in God for your breakthroughs and miracles, amen. Read and study the Word of God; it is true. We serve a God of more than enough. Be blessed today and be a blessing to someone in Jesus' name, amen. Shalom!

26

Blessings and greetings, my caregivers!

As Psalm 136 (KJV) says, "O give thanks unto the Lord, for he is good: and his mercies endureth for ever." We should be grateful for the love of God. God is good all the time. He kept us all, hallelujah; thank You, Lord, for keeping me. When I think about the mere fact that I am alive is enough to shout out loud (thank You, Jesus, thank You, Lord!) for opening my eyes to embrace another day.

Like the little ones you take care of, the ones that feel safe in your arms and smile whenever you are around, do the same in the arms of God. He is not a God far away; He does not want your distance but to be your closest friend and to keep you in joy every day. Caregivers, allow God to guide you, open up your heart and let God take full control of your lives. Stay blessed and focus on Jesus Christ, amen. Shalom!

____

____

____

____

____

____

27

Pleasant morning, greetings, caregivers!

I greet all caregivers in the name of Jesus Christ.

Let's embrace this new day in Jesus' name. "For he is good and his mercy endureth for ever" (Psalm 136, KJV). Let us stay focused on God as never before, for His coming is soon and sure. Abba Father, we thank You. We praise Your Holy name, Jesus! Jesus! Jesus! It feels so good to shout the name of Jesus. Hallelujah, we are alive; thank You, Lord, for sparing our lives. My encouragement today is to stay in the arms of God, and He will wipe all your tears away.

I acknowledge that in this profession, you must have cried sometime. You felt like giving up and walking away. You do not deserve the treatment you receive as an "illegal immigrant." We are all human, and just like any other, we should be treated with respect and love. But when this world does not afford that to us, turn to God.

When this world spits in our faces and laughs at our turmoil, turn to God, the author and finisher of our faith. He is our rock, our shoulder to lean on, and whatever this world throws at us, He is our shield. Hallelujah! Trust God with your heart, and He is going to trust you with the kingdom of heaven, amen! Have a wonderful and Happy day in Jesus' name, amen. Shalom!

____

____

____

____

____

____

28

Shalom, caregivers!

I greet you in the mighty name of Jesus Christ. Hallelujah, I am thankful to God for allowing me to see the beginning of a new day, amen. Remember, we must be born again to enter the kingdom of heaven. Let us prepare in our hearts to meet Jesus Christ, our Savior. It's nice to have Jesus Christ as a friend. Don't allow the distraction of life and the enemies to keep you from serving God, amen.

Trust God with everything you got, and you will not be disappointed. The psalmist wrote, "The sacrifices of God are a broken spirit; a broken and contrite heart, O God, you will not despise" (Psalm 51:17, ESV). God fixes all manner of brokenness in our lives; no matter how big the mountain is, God can bring it down. Jesus' love is everlasting to everlasting.

Are you not excited that someone loves you? I am. Hallelujah, hallelujah, hallelujah, Jesus loves me. Keep on saying it to yourself; man doesn't have to love me; I am more than satisfied knowing that Jesus loves me. Stay encouraged in Jesus' name, amen. Shalom!

___

___

___

___

___

29

Pleasant good morning to all caregivers!

I greet you in the mighty name of Jesus Christ, amen. "Give thanks to the Lord, for he is good! His faithful love endures forever" (Psalm 106:1, NLT), amen. "This is the day the Lord has made. We will rejoice and be glad in it" (Psalm 118:24, NLT), amen. We serve a triune God the Father, God the Son, and God the Holy Spirit, all three in one, amen. Let us approach the throne of grace today and lift up our voices to pray for our caregivers. Let us be each other's keepers. Amen. Without a doubt, by putting God first, we would have a great day in Jesus' name, amen. Shalom!

____

____

____

____

____

____

30

Good morning to all caregivers!

Greetings in the mighty name of Jesus Christ. We serve the only true and living God; it's a privilege to honor Him with praise each day. Hallelujah. I am thankful and grateful for the opportunity to see this day, amen. Let us never take things for granted and prepare our hearts to welcome the King of Glory, Jesus Christ, amen. Caregivers, I want to encourage all of you to put on the entire armor of God.

Let us not be that person who only remembers God when something tragic or good happens. Ephesians 6:10–17 (NLT) explains in detail what the whole armor of God entails. Jesus Christ is our Heavenly Father who loves us unconditionally, allowing Him to work for you. Don't ever run away from God; instead, run to God for everything. I pray that everyone will have a wonderful and blessed weekend with your family in Jesus' name, amen. Shalom!

31

Morning greetings to all caregivers!

God is good, amen! Because of His love and mercies, we are still here. Let us embrace others with love and humbleness, amen. "The stone, the builders, rejected has now become the cornerstone" (Psalm 118:22, NLT). Stay humble, and God is going to uplift you and show you off; believe it, amen. I pray that the overflow of God's blessings be upon each of you and your family in Jesus' name, amen. Shalom!

____

____

____

____

____

____

32

Give thanks, my caregivers!

God is good, amen. Let us all pray, thanking God for another day, amen. I feel happy sharing God's Word daily, amen and hallelujah. We are placed on this Earth to be disciples of Jesus Christ, amen. In times like these, we have to be bold for the things of Christ and stand on God's Word. I would like to encourage someone today to give their life totally to Jesus Christ. I cannot stress enough how important it is to have a relationship with God, amen.

I pray that we all have a wonderful day in Jesus' name, amen. Shalom!

____

____

____

____

____

____

33

An encouragement to all caregivers, in Jesus' name!

The race of life's journey is not only for the swift nor the battle for the strong but for those who endure to the end. For further reading, take time to study Ecclesiastes chapters 11 to 12. My point is, let us all take our time and live a life that is pleasing to God, amen. For one day, this human body has to return to the Earth, amen. The question is, where is our soul going to be? Is it going to be with God or eternal damnation?

I can rightly say our soul should be with God, amen. Let today be the day for change before it's too late. God loves us, and He is waiting with open arms. Accept Jesus today as your personal friend and Savior. Walk with God, talk with God, and tell Him about your trials and tribulations. He is able to fix them, amen. Read and educate yourself about God's Word today, in Jesus' name, amen. Stay blessed. Shalom!

____

____

____

____

____

____

34

Happy morning, caregivers!

Thanks are to God for carrying us through this work week, amen. It is only because of the love of Jesus Christ taking care of us. At one time or another, we may feel that there is no one to turn to, but there is always *God*, amen. Hallelujah! Hallelujah! We always have a friend in Jesus who is always ready to forgive and carry our burdens; God is always there, amen.

Place all your trust in God and let Him work things out on your behalf; in other words, exercise faith. Be encouraged today; Jesus loves us no matter what, amen. Trust God with your heart, and He is going to trust you with the kingdom of heaven, amen. I pray that your days are going to be filled with blessings in Jesus' name, amen. Shalom! List some of your burdens below, and I want you to cross a line through them, symbolizing God erasing them daily and trust that He is and let His will be done.

____

____

____

____

____

____

35

Thanks are to God, all caregivers!

We are making it. I pray that each one of you has a calm and stress-free day, in Jesus' name. Remember who is in control, not you, but God.

Let us pray:

Dear Jesus,

I lift up each caregiver before You this morning; may You give Your angels charge over them in Jesus' name. Whatever they do today, Lord, may Your loving hands guide and protect. Keep their minds and thoughts alert and sharp in Jesus' name. At the end of the day, Father, return them to their respective homes and family safe in Jesus' name, amen. Shalom!

____

____

____

____

____

____

36

Greetings, caregivers, in Jesus' name!

We made it to midweek, amen. God is good, and His mercies endureth for ever and ever, as written in Psalm 136 (KJV), amen. Let us give thanks to God our Heavenly Father for life itself, amen. Personally, I am grateful and thankful for all that God has done and is doing on my behalf. Hallelujah. I discovered years ago the closer you get to God, the better your life gets, amen. So please be encouraged today.

We have a father who loves us no matter what. God is waiting with open arms for us to walk right in, amen. All glory belongs to God for His ever presence. When disappointment comes, brush it aside, and remind yourself there is a reason for every season. Have a beautiful day in Jesus' name, amen. Shalom!

____

____

____

____

____

____

Nurse Anka

Anka migrated to the United States from Poland ten years ago, seeking a better life. I first met Anka when she was working as a housekeeper for a very famous acting couple. She was striding into the Fairway Supermarket on the Upper West Side in New York City. We collided with each other and instantly became friends for life. At that time, she shared with me her story of coming to America pregnant and leaving her husband behind. A few years later, he came and was reunited with his wife and girl child Martha.

Fortunately, Anka's employer later filed papers with immigration for her and her family. She eventually got her citizenship and went to nursing school to become a nurse. During the pandemic, Anka spent almost two years away from home. She later confided how stressful it was holding thousands of patients' hands while they took their last breath. As a Christian, Anka concluded if it was not for God, she would not have made it through. Nurse Anka is only one of the millions of nurses and health care professionals who held it together during the pandemic. May God continue to bless and keep her and her loved ones.

37

Matthew 28:6 (NIV) says, "He is not here; he has risen, just as he has said…" Because of love, many years ago, God gave His only Son, Jesus, to die for our sins, amen. No one will do that for us but *God*. Let us, brothers and sisters, be reminded of who God is in our lives, amen. He is the Alpha and the Omega—the beginning and the end of everything, hallelujah. Today is a reflection of what was and is to come. John 3:16 (KJV) says, "For God so love the world, that he gave his only begotten Son, that whosoever believeth in him should not perish but have everlasting life." Amen.

This promise of our Savior reminds us that it doesn't matter where we have been or what we may have done and are facing at this very moment. Jesus Christ is our only hope, amen. We are no longer under guilt and shame; we are a new person in Jesus Christ. Glory be to God. Thank You, Lord, for Your resurrection power. Thank You, Jesus, for dying for us. You are the victorious King of Glory; You live forever and ever. I pray that we keep God at the forefront of our thoughts and in everything that we do. Be blessed in Jesus' name, amen. Shalom!

____

____

____

____

____

38

Happy day to my caregivers!

Thanks are to God for keeping us, amen. Step into your blessings in Jesus' name. We have the authority given to us by God to make declarations over everything in our lives. Amen. It doesn't matter what we may need help with, trust and believe that all things are possible in Jesus' name. I declare and decree that all needs will be met today in Jesus' name, amen. I pray that all situations will be rectified in Jesus' name. As we all begin this work week, I pray that our Heavenly Father grants us strength, courage, and endurance in Jesus' mighty name, amen. Shalom!

____

____

____

____

____

____

39

Blessed morning to all caregivers, in Jesus' name!

The psalmist says in Psalm 1:1–3 that we should meditate on God's Word day and night, amen. We should *not* call on God *only* when we are faced with situations and problems, amen. In everything, we should give thanks to the LORD, amen. It's already done; the price for all of our sins was paid for at Calvary cross, amen. Do *you* not feel good knowing that someone loves you *so* much that He has given His life for you? I am forever humbled by Your *love*, LORD. Let us take a moment and renew our faith in God, amen. Hallelujah, it's a new day; walk into your *victory* in Jesus' name, amen. Shalom!

____

____

____

____

____

____

40

Happy day, caregivers!

Blessings upon blessings in Jesus' name. As I was studying the Bible at around 4:17 a.m., I felt a great joy fill my heart. Caregivers, the Word of God has power, amen. As I read the book of *Ecclesiastes*, chapter 3 tells of "a season" (please study). Each one of us may be going through a tough season, but it will not last forever. Hallelujah! After your season, there will be your harvest, amen. Put all of your trust in God because you are coming into your harvest, amen. I am excited for all my caregivers in Christ, don't be afraid to claim what is rightfully yours, amen. God loves you, and Jesus is the Lord. Have a wonderful day in Jesus' name, amen. Shalom!

41

Good morning, caregivers!

Pull out your Bible, caregivers in Christ, read and meditate on God's Word, amen. On the day of judgment, we all will have to answer to God for the choices we make, amen. Let us not harden our hearts, freely give it to your Heavenly Father, and your rewards will be greater, amen. I pray that the day is filled with peace, joy, and total happiness in Jesus' name, amen. Shalom! What scripture did you study this morning? Write down your thoughts on this scripture and meditate on it throughout your day while doing your service.

____

____

____

____

____

____

42

Pleasant day, all caregivers!

If you have made it to the end of another work day or week, thanks are to God, amen. Let us keep looking ahead, knowing that Jesus Christ is our provider. I would like to encourage you, yes you, to make God your main source of provision, amen. He is our provider; He is our healer; God is our everything, amen.

Sometimes in our lives, doubt tries to creep in, don't allow doubt to take root in your heart, amen. I live by these Bible verses "I can do all things through Christ who strengthens me" (Philippians 4:13, NKJV). Encourage yourself and others; we are our brother's keeper, amen. I pray that you and your family have a wonderful and blessed weekend in Jesus' almighty name, amen. Shalom!

____

____

____

____

____

____

43

Brothers and sisters in Christ, let us open up our mouths and intercede with prayers on behalf of everyone in countries that are being ravaged by natural disasters. The forces of Mother Nature raise its head. We speak to volcanoes, earthquakes, tsunamis, floods, cyclones, and hurricanes, be *calm* and *still* in Jesus' name. To the people who are directly affected or their relatives back home, be of good courage.

The Bible says, "Weeping may endure for the night, but joy cometh in the morning" (Psalm 30:5, KJV). Remember these people in your prayers today, amen. Thank You, Lord, for working on those natural events right now and protecting Your people, in Jesus' almighty name, amen. Shalom!

____

____

____

____

____

____

44

Here are your day's blessings, caregivers!

Rise up, caregivers, and find your peace in Jesus Christ, amen. The power was given to us by our Heavenly Father to conquer the Earth. Whatever the need you may have today, place it at Jesus' feet, amen. I am so happy to be able to share the *Word* of God; I am here to encourage, not to discourage, amen. This morning I prayed over all caregivers in whatever capacity they may serve in Jesus' name.

I pray that the window of heaven will open in their lives and God will pour out blessings upon blessings in Jesus' name. Receive your blessings, hallelujah. Open your mouths and claim your blessings in Jesus' name. Say, "Father, I receive Your blessings in Jesus' name. I thank You, Lord, for loving us, for always providing for us, for always healing us, for forgiving all of our sins, in Jesus' name." I have experienced God's love in every area of my life, amen. Be encouraged today in Jesus' mighty name, amen. Shalom!

____

____

____

____

____

____

45

Caregivers

Thank God we're in the land of the living caregivers, amen.

Even when the day is rough, God makes it easy, amen. Glory be to God, for He is good to all of us, and His mercies are ever extended, amen. As I was doing my Bible studies early this morning, I began to meditate on God's Word. I felt a calmness and peace take over me, amen.

I want to let the world know that the *Spirit* of the Lord brings joy, amen (Ecclesiastes chapters 5 to 8). Whether rich or poor, we *can* experience the love of our Father, amen. I pray over families today in the name of Jesus. Put all of your trust in God; He is more than able to take care of all of us in Jesus' mighty name, amen. I pray that your day is peaceful and productive in Jesus' almighty name, amen. Shalom!

____

____

____

____

____

____

46

Happy day to all caregivers, in Jesus' name!

It is the start of a new work day; praise be to God. Let us all embrace what God has in store for each of us, amen. I pray blessings upon blessings come our way in Jesus' name. As responsible adults, let us ask ourselves this question. If God was to come at this very moment, would we be ready? The answer for some would be, "I need more time." John's vision in the book of Revelation is proven to be the true revelation of God.

Jesus Christ is coming again soon. But according to the Bible, He shall come like a thief in the night. This simply means *no* one will know exactly the day, the hour, or the minute God is going to appear. But the world will know in an instant when He bursts through the sky to receive His own. The good news is that *now* we have the time to prepare ourselves to meet God, amen.

The signs and wonders are here; study the Bible because God's Word is *true*, amen. Let us keep our hearts on God and the things of God, amen. Let us prepare ourselves to meet God, amen. I trust that these words will encourage you in the mighty name of Jesus Christ, amen. Shalom!

47

Blessings to all caregivers, in Jesus' name!

How to claim your inheritance?

You may be asking yourself, "Inheritance?" Yes, I say "inheritance." We are citizens of the kingdom of God, remember! And we all have an inheritance. Whatever we say or do determines when or how we may lay claim to our inheritance, amen. Our Heavenly Father has an inheritance for us; we were created in the image and likeness of God (read and study the book of Genesis); since we are all children of the highest God, we have inherited an inheritance, amen.

This is a hallelujah moment; God wants to bless you today, hallelujah, hallelujah. Please, don't run away from God, but run to Him. Confess your sins, and give your life totally to God. Accept Jesus Christ as your Lord and Savior. The past will be washed away; all things will be made new. Caregivers, start enjoying your inheritance here on Earth until you can claim your rewards in heaven.

According to Matthew chapter 18, we were given the keys to the kingdom of God. Proverbs 18:21 (KJV) also says, "Life and death are in the power of the tongue," we have the power to change our circumstances. I want to encourage you and myself today to be strong in the Lord and don't be afraid to claim your inheritance in Jesus' name, amen. Shalom!

____

____

____

____

____

____

48

Good morning, caregivers!

Let's pray.

Heavenly Father,

Thank You for another day. Thank You for waking me up this morning. Thank You for loving me. Come into my heart, Lord, and change me from the inside out. I belong to You, Lord. Have Your way in my life, forgive me of all my wrongdoing, make me a new person in Jesus' name, amen.

Caregivers, you could add to this simple prayer as you see fit and what you ask for, do it in the name of Jesus, amen. We don't have to go before God with big words but with simple words, sincerely from our hearts. Psalm 51:17 says, "A broken and contrite heart God will not despise," amen. Don't worry if you have never cried out to God before; make some time each day for God, amen. God is always there, waiting for us to recognize and honor Him. Talk to Him as you would any friend. Sisters, we are absolutely nothing without God, hallelujah.

Put God first in everything you do, and He would put you first in the heavenly places, amen. Jesus loves us so much if we can only see it. My plea today is to *try* Jesus today, and there would be no regrets. Have a wonderful day in Jesus' mighty name, amen. Shalom!

____

____

____

____

____

____

49

Thank you, God, for keeping us!

Another day of thanksgiving, amen. We have so many things to thank God for our health, the breath in our lungs, the food on our table, our family and friends, our jobs, just think about everything and give thanks, amen. I thank God for the opportunity to see another sunrise, for the wisdom to share the *Word* of Jesus Christ, and for all of the additional blessings, hallelujah! I am grateful to Abba Father.

I get overwhelmed just thinking about the goodness of God in my life. Thank You, Jesus, thank You, Lord, for loving me even when I don't deserve it. Caregivers, throughout your day, just thank God, thank Him for what He has done and is about to do in your life, don't give up; He is working it out, amen. I want to share something: Your miracles from God are already here, but because we lose faith in God, it has not materialized, amen.

Hang on to the hem of Jesus' garment and place all of your trust in Him, amen. I pray over your families in the name of Jesus Christ. Have a truly blessed and wonderful day/weekend in Jesus' name, amen. Shalom!

____

____

50

Praise the Lord, caregivers!

We are here because of God's grace. Another day, thank you, Jesus, amen. I am encouraging you this morning to continue having faith in Jesus Christ. All your needs and wants shall be met in Jesus' name. First Peter 5:7 (KJV) says, "Casting all your care upon him; for he careth for you." This scripture is simply telling us not to worry; God got us, amen. Have a wonderful and productive day in Jesus' mighty name, amen. Shalom! What cares do you have on your mind today? Write them down, tear out the page if you have to, and give it to Jesus.

____

____

____

____

____

____

51

Pleasant good morning, caregivers, in Jesus' name!

What is endurance? The Webster Dictionary says, "Endurance is the ability to sustain prolonged or stressful effort." In simple words, it's the ability to hang in there when things get rough or tough. Ecclesiastes 9:11 (KJV) says, "[…] the race is not to the swift, nor the battle to the strong…" The author is referring to the race of life; there will be trials and tribulations but don't give up, amen.

We are to hang in there whenever we feel like giving up. God, in His timing, is working it out for our good. Sisters, my encouragement today is don't murmur or stress about anything; God is in control, hallelujah, amen. Don't matter what comes your way today; Jesus loves you. Have a wonderful day in Jesus' name, amen. Shalom!

____

____

____

____

____

____

52

Blessings, caregivers!

Let us not forget to make Jesus Christ the Lord of our lives, amen. When we do that, God's blessings are in abundance. I want to encourage each caregiver to have faith in Jesus Christ. In this life, we were meant to be happy and prosperous, trust God and allow Him to work miracles on your behalf.

Always remember God is always good, with everlasting mercies. Today don't let the enemy distract you from the things of God, amen. Caregivers, hold your heads up high; our Heavenly Father loves you and wants to bless you, amen. In everything you do today, stay connected to God and allow Him to bless you in Jesus' mighty name, amen. Shalom!

____

____

____

____

____

____

53

Happy morning, caregivers!

I greet each and everyone in the mighty name of Jesus Christ, amen. Let us thank God for another day, amen. When I think about the goodness of God and all that He has done for me, I don't have a choice but to say, "Thank You, Abba Father." Wherever you may be in your walk with God, always remember that God loves us all, amen. Today is a new day, caregivers; claim your blessings in Jesus' name. Amen.

Let us pray.

Jesus, we thank You for Your mercies and Your grace. We thank You, Lord, for sparing our lives to see another day, amen. Continue to direct the paths of all caregivers in Jesus' name. Abba Father, we thank You for loving us and working out everything for our good, amen.

Because of God's love, we can face anything and accomplish everything in Jesus' name. Keep the love of Jesus Christ flowing in your hearts as you maneuver your daily duties in Jesus' mighty name, amen. Shalom!

54

Blessed morning, caregivers!

Let us scream it out, "God is good!" Amen.

I feel happy knowing that Jesus loves all of us today and always, amen. Take some time and just bask in Jesus' love, hallelujah! Feel His protected arms wrap around you, and whatever burden you may be carrying, let it go, amen. Jesus' love is sweeter than any earthly love, amen. Be encouraged today in Jesus' name, amen. Shalom! I will give you a moment to meditate.

____

____

____

____

____

____

Amiga

I met Amiga on the street of New York City; she works as a nanny. When we met, she said it was God's doing. She said, "*Hola!*" and I said "*Hola!*" to her in return. While talking to her, I commented on the sad look of her eyes; she immediately broke into tears. Alarmed, I asked her if I had said something wrong. With her limited ability to speak English, she said no. We quickly found a corner, and she shared her story. She is from Ecuador; fifteen years ago, by foot, she and her husband Amigo set off to find the American dream. It took them almost a year on their journey, leaving behind her four young children with relatives.

She began to weep, which really touched my heart. Her problem was that the children left behind are now adults but were denied a visa into the United States on several occasions. She said thanks to WhatsApp and Zoom, she can video call, but it's not the same. During the pandemic, braving the onslaught of the virus, she still had to work as a nanny/housekeeper for the rich and famous. The daily encouragement I send her gives her hope that one day a miracle will happen, and things will get better in Jesus' name.

55

Good morning and blessings, caregivers, in Jesus' name!

I want to encourage all caregivers today to hang in there, don't give up, amen. There may be unbearable situations you are facing, but trust God; He is willing and able to pull you through, amen. Jesus Christ is our supplier, amen. Let me repeat this; God is our supplier, amen. This is a hallelujah moment, knowing we can place every situation in God's hand, amen.

Today, we give thanks to our Lord and Savior, Jesus Christ, for *His* promises and love. Philippians 4:19 (NASB) said, "My God will supply all your needs according to all His riches in glory." God's Word is true, so continue trusting God for everything, amen. Have a wonderful day in Jesus' name, amen. Shalom! Ask for what you want today.

____

____

____

____

____

____

56

Good morning, caregivers!

Thanks are to God, amen.

My encouragement today is for you to keep on trusting God for everything in your life. Challenging times will come, but continue praising God. Spend more time in the *Word* of God and watch the miracles happen in your lives. Remember, the best is yet to come, amen. Mothers are special in God's eyes. Today, I am especially setting aside this time to celebrate the women who reproduced and took care of their offspring(s).

The scripture honors women today, reaching out to another woman and letting her know how special she is. Jesus, bless and keep all the mothers whose work is never-ending. Give them the strength and endurance to raise up a good family in the fear of the Lord. Embrace your day with *love*. Have a wonderful, beautiful day in Jesus' name, amen. Shalom!

____

____

____

____

____

____

57

Happy day to all caregivers!

By God's grace, we are still here, amen. God is good, amen. (Let me repeat.) God is great, hallelujah.

Let us pray.

Heavenly Father,

I thank You for loving us. I thank You for providing for us. You have been and will always be a good, good father whose love never fails, amen. Continue to bless us in tremendous ways because You are a big and generous God, amen. Bless and keep all caregivers and me safe today and always in Jesus' name, amen. Shalom!

Say your prayer:

____

____

____

____

____

____

58

God's blessing to all caregivers!

For this morning's encouragement, I want to share how happy I feel today, knowing that Jesus Christ is my friend and Savior. It doesn't matter where you are in your walk with God; always remember God is love. God never judges, criticizes, or condemns us. His *love* is unconditional, amen. When you go before God, confessing your sins, asking Him to wash you, and making you new, it's done.

Today I want to encourage caregivers to draw closer to God. Everything that was lost or taken away from me was restored when I made Jesus Christ my Lord and Savior. Glory be to God, hallelujah. Trust God for your breakthrough in Jesus' name, amen. Shalom!

____

____

____

____

____

____

59

It is a wonderful day, caregivers!

Thank God, our Heavenly Father is and has been good to all of us, amen. I trust that God will continue to strengthen us in our spiritual walk with Him. Don't ever allow the enemy to prevail, put God first. When doubts pop up, use scripture-filled words like these to get rid of him. "I can do all things through Christ who strengthens me" (Philippians 4:13, KJV). There is a scripture in the Holy Bible for every season in our lives.

Ephesians 6 encourages us to put on the full armor of God, amen. Despite the many situations in our lives, we should be glad, always. Allow me to remind you why we woke up this morning and have breath in our lungs, plus all the other added blessings; it was because of God's love. This is a hallelujah moment; thank You, Lord.

All praises belong to God, for God is good "and his mercies endureth forever" (Psalm 136, NKJV), amen. Today be confident in Jesus Christ, amen. Let your light shine before the world. Stay rooted and grounded in the Lord and Savior Jesus Christ, amen. Shalom!

____

____

____

____

60

Good morning, caregivers!

Our Heavenly Father has kept us, amen. Let us give God a huge shout-out right now, thanking Him for all that He has done and is about to do in our lives, amen. Be encouraged, caregivers; the best is yet to come; glory be to God. If you have problems, take them to God in prayer. If you need a job or a better job, take it to God in prayer.

If you need a good husband, take it to God in prayer. Anything and everything is yours right now in the name of Jesus. As I was studying the Word of God last night, a message came for me to share, amen. God wants His saints to know that we are living in the last days, and we must never allow the devil to shut us up.

Don't be afraid to shout and praise God anywhere and anytime, amen. We have dominion over everything on this Earth. You may ask, "Who? Am I?" Yes, you. You are children of the highest God and were given permission and authority by the true and living God, Jesus Christ. Caregivers, have a wonderful and blessed weekend in Jesus' mighty name, amen. Shalom! Which scripture are you going to share with others today?

61

Good morning, caregivers!

“This is the day the Lord has made; We shall rejoice and be glad in it” (Psalm 118:24, NKJV). Blessed Monday to all my caregiver sisters. It is the beginning of a new work week, amen. Let us be grateful and thankful to God for keeping us, amen. I am happy and blessed that God kept all of us in Jesus’ name. Be encouraged, do all that must be done because your Heavenly Father is on your side, amen.

I pray for all caregivers in the name of Jesus; I pray that your day proceeds peacefully, stress-free, and with joy in Jesus’ name. I pray for all the caregivers who may not have a job at this moment; it is coming in Jesus’ name, have faith. Have a wonderful day, in Jesus’ mighty name, amen. Shalom!

____

____

____

____

____

____

62

Praise the Lord!

Pleasant morning to caregivers.

My message today is that God is taking you somewhere.

Today, just think about where you want to be in your lives. Wherever you want to go in life can only be fulfilled by putting *God* first, amen. Caregivers, all of the storehouses of heaven are yours for the taking; just trust God, amen. "Love the Lord your God with all your heart and with all your soul and with all your mind" (Matthew 22:37, NIV). And throughout the Bible, you will find scriptures to confirm it. Today is the day to claim your inheritance in Jesus' name, amen. Shalom!

____

____

____

____

____

____

63

Good morning, caregivers!

"If My people who are called by My name will humble themselves, and pray and seek My face, and turn from their wicked ways, then I would hear from heaven, and will forgive their sins and heal their land" (2 Chronicles 7:14, NKJV). This world is in need of prayers, our prayers. We have to intercede on behalf of the people of this Earth, amen. Everywhere you turn, there is turmoil and confusion. (Read and study the book of Revelation.)

The Bible must be fulfilled, amen. I want to encourage you sisters to partition with me before God. Let us bring whatever is happening before our Heavenly Father's throne; God answers prayers, amen. Let us not forget whatever we ask, we must ask in the name of Jesus, and it shall be done. Who will help me pray? Would it be you?

May God bless and keep you always, in Jesus' name, amen. Shalom!

____

____

____

____

____

____

64

Happy morning to all caregivers!

I trust that all of you had a wonderful weekend like myself, amen. I pray that these words will encourage you today as you walk with God. The Word of God and the knowledge of God are powerful. There are no longer any limits to what the children of God can do in this world because Jesus Christ gives Christians the ability to do all things. Without Christ, you are faced with limitations: sin, fear, sicknesses, infirmities, challenges, death, and the like. However, when Jesus Christ comes into your life, He gives you grace to overcome all of these. Apostle Paul knew this secret, and therefore he declared, "I can do all things through Christ who strengthens me." Whenever you face any limitation, declare the same words as Paul: "I can do all things through Christ who strengthens me" (Philippians 4:13, KJV). As you continue to declare this, the limitation will vanish. Hallelujah. Caregivers, are you confronted with any limitations? Place them in the hands of our Heavenly Father. Have a great and Blessed day, in Jesus' name, amen. Shalom!

____

____

____

____

____

65

Blessed morning to all caregivers!

Do you know what love is? Do we really love and care for one another? The Bible said we must love one another as we love ourselves with any great examples of acts of love, amen. As Christians, we must first look at the word *love* from a biblical perspective. Love is an emotion felt and action performed by someone concerned for the well-being of someone else. The first act of true love was shown by our triune God. Godhead—Father, Son, Jesus, and the Holy Spirit.

Love is not a personal sexual satisfaction given or received from or by someone. Love is not sometimes convenient; love is not temporary. Love is forever. The Hebrew word *chesed* or the Greek word *agape* explains more about true, genuine love. John 3:16 (KJV) stated, "For God so love the world, that he gave his only begotten Son, that whosoever believeth in him, should not perish, but have everlasting life."

Caregivers, let us examine our hearts and let go of anything and everything that may prevent us from loving the godly way, amen. I love each and every one of you with the love of Christ, have a great day in Jesus' name, amen. Shalom!

____

____

____

____

____

66

Midweek blessings to all caregivers!

Thanks are to God for keeping us, amen. Continue in your prayerfulness, holding on to Jesus Christ. God is our rock and will always protect us if we allow Him to. Caregivers, be encouraged, don't give up, even when things seem impossible, amen. Stand on your faith in Jesus Christ. Whatever worries that may be trying to interrupt your godly thought, cast them aside in the name of Jesus.

Lay all of life's problems at Jesus' feet. I always say, "Why worry about things when God is taking care of everything?" Caregivers, in this earthly life, trust God with your whole heart, for and with everything, amen. As we go about our daily lives today, I want you to always keep God at the center of everything. Have a truly Blessed day in Jesus' mighty name, amen. Shalom!

67

Thank You, Lord, for keeping us!

Good morning and blessings, caregivers!

God is a kind and merciful God, amen. Thank You, Jesus, for loving us. Caregivers continue to stay in the presence of God and don't ever stray away. Life's distractions can cause us to shift our focus sometimes, but allow faith in God to lead you to your destiny, amen. Let us continue to make memories with each other, in love, peace, and harmony, in Jesus' name. Praise ye the Lord.

"Oh give thanks unto God; for he is good: For his mercy endureth forever" (Psalm 106, KJV). Lord, I lift all the caregivers of this world. Lord, You protect them and their loved ones in Jesus' name. Jesus, please continue to provide and supply all their needs in this time, and we receive all Your blessings today in Jesus' mighty name, amen. Shalom!

____

____

____

____

____

____

68

Good morning, caregivers!

Great is the faithfulness of God towards us. Gracious morning to all caregivers.

We serve a faithful God; are we faithful to God? Many times we give up too easily. We may be praying for something or about something, and too quickly, we are ready to throw in the towel. What we must always remember is that God does everything at the right time, amen.

Philippians 4:19 (KJV) says, "But my God will supply all of your needs, according to his riches in glory by Christ Jesus." This is a hallelujah moment right there, amen. So today, whatever you may be trusting God for, don't give up. God's blessings are limitless, amen. Trust God with your whole heart, and wait for His blessings in Jesus' name, amen. Shalom!

____

____

____

____

____

____

69

Blessed day to all caregivers!

Would you stand up for Jesus Christ?

"I will praise thee, O LORD, among the people: and I will sing praises unto thee among the nations" (Psalm 108:3, KJV). Caregivers, there are persons who feel ashamed about letting others know that they are Christians. Others will only hold their Bible in church or at home. As Christians, we should be proud to stand boldly and publicly for the One who hung unashamed on a wooden cross for us.

If Jesus did it for us, we can be like the psalmist and publicly sing praises to God. Caregivers, it doesn't matter where we are; let us give God the praise. Put your shame aside. Let the world know that you serve the true and living God. The times we are living in call for the body of the church to get radical for God. Rejoice in the Lord, hallelujah! Today is the day, caregivers, for us all to stand up for Jesus Christ, amen.

God has been keeping us, protecting us, providing for us, and healing us. If you have not done so already, please stand up for Jesus today. May the saving grace of Lord and Savior Jesus Christ bless and keep us, amen. Shalom!

70

Good morning, caregivers!

"Behold, I am the LORD, the God of all flesh: is there anything too hard for me?" (Jeremiah 32:27, KJV)

Gracious day to all caregivers.

Nothing is impossible with God. Our God, who created the heavens and the Earth and everything within it, is asking a question in Jeremiah. I agree at times, things in life can be a bit of a challenge or even unbearable. But God wants us to stand strong. He doesn't want us to focus on our circumstances. Instead, He wants us to keep our focus on Him, amen. Remember, "[…] with God all things are possible" (Matthew 19:26, NIV).

Caregivers, no matter what you may be experiencing at the moment, don't allow it to distract you from focusing on God. He can and will do the impossible for you. Trust God with your whole heart, and He will trust you with the key to the kingdom of heaven. I pray that each and every one who reads these encouraging words finds peace in Jesus Christ, amen. Shalom!

71

Happy day, caregivers!

"Then he said unto them, Go your way, eat the fat, and drink the sweet, and send portions unto them for whom nothing is prepared: for this day is holy unto our Lord: neither be ye sorry; for the joy of the LORD is your strength" (Nehemiah 8:10, KJV). Caregivers, God does not want you to cry or weep at hearing His Word.

At times, yes, we may get emotional in a happy way, and tears may flow. But God wants for all of us to rejoice in His Word and gain strength by it. When we celebrate the Word of God, His strength will be imparted to you, amen. With God's happiness, His strength is then released upon us to function in His kingdom. Caregivers, make the Lord's joy your strength today, amen. Blessings and God's protection upon you and your family in Jesus' name, amen. Shalom!

____

____

____

____

____

____

72

Pleasant day, caregivers!

Greetings in the wonderful name of Jesus Christ. As we begin a new work day, always remember nothing is impossible with God. "And he said, The things which are impossible with men are possible with God" (Luke 18:27, KJV). You may be like the young rich ruler holding on to material things in this life. How many times have you passed that homeless person on the street, turning up your nose in disgust?

If God was to ask you to share the things you love the most with them, would you do it? Don't be like that rich young ruler in the scripture and cling onto earthly treasures. It is better to build treasures in heaven than on Earth. God doesn't care about the fancy cars, clothing, or what type of house you live in. He cares about our hearts, amen. Caregivers, no situation is impossible with God; with men, it is impossible but not with God. Trust God for the impossible, amen.

Let us pray.

Heavenly Father,

This morning, I pray for all caregivers. I pray that their faith in Jesus Christ is renewed and refreshed daily; I pray that their riches are in Christ Jesus. Keep and protect them all in Jesus' name, amen. Shalom!

____

____

____

____

____

____

Ms. Monica

Always smiling, once lived in Brooklyn, New York, and worked in Manhattan. Considered an elder, she migrated from Dominica twelve years ago. Grounded in the Lord, she was loved and admired by all. Working as a nanny/governess, she fell ill in March 2020. Ms. Monica had lots of future plans. One of them was to retire in the next three years and return to her country to start her Christian ministry. All the money she was working for went into building her dream home back in her country. What was very strange was that the family she worked for had traveled to Europe and returned sick with flu-like symptoms. They took themselves and their kids to the doctor. Monica kept on giving medicine to the children until she became sick herself.

One day a mutual friend called me and asked me to plead with Ms. Monica to go see the doctor. After barely hearing her speak between taking breaths, I pleaded with her to go to the hospital. She eventually went, and days later, her test came back positive for COVID-19. A few days after she died. That's when a lot of close friends and family of Monica realized COVID-19 was deadly. Sometimes I wonder if a lot of people died because of the virus itself or lack of care; only God knows.

73

Good morning, all caregivers!

My question this morning is, how strong is your spiritual foundation? Luke 6:48 (KJV) says, "He is like a man who built a house, and dug deep, and laid the foundation on a rock: and when the flood arose, the stream beat vehemently upon that house, and could not shake it: for it was founded upon a rock."

Another provoking question came to mind: Are we, as believers, hearing the Word of God daily but not following what the Word says? Then we are building our spiritual foundation on soft mud. One day we listen to what God's Word says, but eventually, it goes out of the other ear. Jesus was illustrating how He wants us as Christians to be. He wants us to be like the wise builder so that when the trials of life come, we can stand strong on the Word of God, amen. Jesus Christ is our rock.

Caregivers, the only spiritual foundation you should be building your life on is the living Word of God. It doesn't matter what storms and floods of life come your way; you will withstand and surely succeed. I trust that these words will make you think about your life and where you would like to spend eternity. Jesus is the only way; stay blessed in Jesus Christ, amen. Shalom!

74

God's blessings, caregivers!

"I will say of the LORD, He is my refuge and my fortress: my God; in him will I trust" (Psalm 91:2, KJV). I greet my sisters this morning in the wonderful, mighty name of Jesus Christ. Is God first place in your life? The answer is: We should always put God first, amen. Yes, we all may have a busy or hectic day. But make that special effort and set aside some time for God. Tell Him about everything, don't forget to give Him thanks for everything, amen.

When we pray to ask God for things, we must believe that it is done, amen. Caregivers, all we have is Jesus Christ. When everything fails, God never fails. His promise is always yes, and amen. Today, please make time for God because He always makes time for you. May the blessings of Abraham be upon us all, in Jesus' name, amen. Shalom!

____

____

____

____

____

____

75

Blessed greetings to all caregivers!

God is great, amen. I must repeat myself, God is great and awesome in power, amen. Caregivers, do you know that God thinks about each and every one of us? Jeremiah 29:11 (KJV) says it best, "For I know the thoughts that I think toward you, saith the Lord, thoughts of peace, and not of evil, to give you an expected end." As any good Father, God, in His creative way, has a very good plan for each of us, and this is demonstrated by His thoughts toward us. God doesn't just give us a plan without showing us how to set it up. In fact, He is the planner of all planners.

When God sets a plan in motion, it is well done, amen. Let us look at it this way: God is the master architect. Caregivers, you are part of God's plan. Let us murmur not or complain because, at the end of our time on this Earth, we are going to hear our Heavenly Father say: "Well done." Caregivers, be convinced of God's plan for your life. I pray that knowing that God has a plan for all of us should keep us happy and, in everything, enjoy what life has to offer. Stay in faith, trust God at His Word, and have a beautiful day in Jesus' name, amen. Shalom!

76

Pleasant morning, caregivers!

Thank God we woke up this morning. It was only by God's grace, amen.

"Let them give thanks unto the Lord, for his unfailing love and His wonderful deeds for mankind, for he satisfies the thirsty and fills the hungry with good things" (Psalm 107:8–9, NIV). We serve a God who loves us unconditionally. His promises are always yes, and amen. Are we hungry for the manifestation of God's generosity? Our answer should unequivocally be yes.

Caregivers, we must constantly remind ourselves daily that we can do all things because God loves us. Even though life's trials and temptations may come our way, that does not mean we should give up. That is the time when we have to take everything to God in prayer. Let's face today with a positive attitude because God's got us in the palm of His hands, amen. Have a wonderful day in Jesus' name, amen. Shalom!

77

Good morning encouragement to all caregivers!

Invitation!

Let's "enter his gates with thanksgiving and his courts with praise; give thanks to him and praise his [holy] name" (Psalm 100:4, NIV). We all have been kept and will continue to be kept by God, amen. Once there is breath in our lungs, we should be thankful and give God all the glory. Abba Father has always been merciful, loving, and kind to us all. Warning! But the enemy is always watching and waiting to steal from you. He wants to steal your joy and happiness, your health and healing, wealth and financial overflow, your children, your marriage, your friends, and the list continues.

But stop! It can only happen if we allow him to. Proverbs 18:21 (KJV) says that the power of life and death is in the tongue. Caregivers, open up your mouths today and make declarations over everything in your lives. Cover everything that is concerning you with Jesus's shed blood. Sing to God even when you don't feel like singing, don't allow circumstances to take over your thoughts, amen. You have the Holy Spirit dwelling inside of you, working on your behalf.

Let us pray:

I pray this morning, Lord, that You will use all the hard-working caregivers in mighty and bountiful ways. Continue to bless them in Jesus' name. May the blessings of Abraham be upon each of them in Jesus' mighty name, amen. Shalom!

____

____

____

____

____

____

78

Pleasant morning, caregivers!

I greet each of you in the wonderful name of Jesus Christ, amen.

As I was studying the *Word* of God this morning, a question came to mind: As servants of God, are we obedient to Him? The gospel of John depicts many theological aspects of the Son of God. On one occasion, Mary, Jesus' chosen earthly mother, was with Him and His disciples at a wedding in Cana of Galilee. The wine ran out. "His mother saith unto the servants, Whatsoever he [Jesus] saith unto you, do it" (John 2:5, KJV), and they were.

This little example signifies as much; we are to be good servants, amen. Caregivers, let's examine ourselves; let us go before God today, asking for a servant's heart and the right spirit. "God is a Spirit: and they that worship him must worship him in spirit and in truth" (John 4:24, KJV). God wants and deserves total obedience from us. Stay safe and blessed in Jesus' name, amen. Shalom!

____

____

____

____

____

____

79

Good morning, caregivers!

It is a beautiful day in Christ Jesus, amen. There is so much God has in store for us; His storehouse is unlimited. We just have to place all of our faith in Him (God) and take Him at His word. The Bible says,

> Don't worry about anything; instead, pray about everything. Tell God what you need, and thank Him for all he has done. Then you will experience God's peace, which exceeds anything we can understand. His peace will guard your hearts and minds as you live in Christ Jesus.

Philippians 4:6–7 (NLT)

Caregivers, today is your day for limitless blessings in the Lord. Surround yourself with God's love and allow Him to bless you in every possible way. Have a wonderful day with your loved ones in Jesus' name, amen. Shalom!

80

Happy day, caregivers!

The Word of God says, "And you yourself must be an example to them by doing good works of every kind. Let everything you do reflect the integrity and seriousness of your teaching" (Titus 2:7, NLT). Caregivers, as Christians, we are the light of the world, and in whatever area of caregiving, the best is expected of us. When we do our jobs, we do our best, even when circumstances may not be fair. As believers, we must be guided by the good work of Jesus Christ. That's why it is important to spend quality time studying the Word of God and incorporating it into your daily life. The most important thing is we don't have to twist the Word of God; quote it as is, in all honesty, and with great sincerity. God's Word is true; no need to dilute or add corrections.

Remember what Proverbs 18:21 (KJV) says, "Death and life are in the power of the tongue…." The tongue may be one of the softest parts of our body, but it carries a lot of weight. By doing our good works and using our words positively, we will put our enemies to shame. Caregivers, it is possible to leave a good legacy for the world to copy. Let us all stay focused on God's Word in Jesus' name, amen. Shalom! What legacy do you desire to leave behind?

81

Pleasant Morning greetings to all caregivers!

What a wonderful day to wake up and give the Lord all the praise, amen. "He has made everything beautiful in His time" (Ecclesiastes 3:11, ESV). I remember times in the past when these words and scripture would cause me much doubt. Reading these words in difficult moments, I would think, God of heaven, how can this be beautiful? How can times of grief, tragedy, and moments of loss ever be seen in a good light?

In the midst of my pain and distrust, my daughter gives birth to a handsome baby boy. While holding my grandson on my chest for the first time, I took a moment to think; amid the pain, here comes happiness and joy. I began to read and study the Gospel of John, the narrative of the man who, for thirty-eight years, was paralyzed. (Please, read John chapter 5.) One day Jesus stops by and asks him if he would like to be made well. After the man explained his position, he was healed; please, refer to John 5:1–4 (NIV).

The answer is God makes all things beautiful. So no matter where you are today or what you may be going through, God will make beauty out of it. Caregivers, we serve a beautiful God who loves us unconditionally, amen. We are beautiful caregivers with a purpose guided by Christ's love, amen. Shalom! Remember that moment God showed beauty to you in the midst of your pain.

____

____

____

____

____

____

82

Your daily thanksgiving, caregivers!

This morning, “Let us come before his presence with thanksgiving, and make a joyful noise unto him with psalms” (Psalm 95:2, KJV). Caregivers, we should be thankful for every opportunity given to us on Earth by God. Sometimes we may find ourselves getting overwhelmed by situations. But by trusting God, everything gets fixed in Jesus’ name. The Bible tells us about a man named Job, who lost everything he had: wife, children, wealth, health, and everything else. He remained by himself many times the devil showed up, telling him to curse God and die. But he did not give in; he placed all of his trust in God. Even when sores came out all over his body, he kept on praising God. And because he did not give up everything, more was restored unto him abundantly.

Caregivers, let us be tough together. Let us be like Job; no matter what comes our way, we are not going to give up, amen. I remembered so many years ago that my new-born daughter passed away. I sat for a long time, just hold-ing her in my arms, heartbroken; I was overwhelmed with grief. At that moment, I would trade everything to see her chest rise and fall. Sadly, my mother-in-law passed away a few weeks later. But I did not give up on my Lord, and my tears were wiped away. I felt better knowing that they both were resting in Christ, amen.

How many of us today are like Job? My message today is to hold on and keep on thanking God. Your breakthrough is here, amen. I pray that God is going to bless all caregivers in Jesus' name, amen. Shalom!

____

____

____

____

____

____

83

Great morning, caregivers!

"And if those days [of tribulation] had not been cut short, no human life will be saved; but for the sake of the elect (God's chosen ones) those days will be shortened" (Matthew 24:22, AMP). Sisters, let us prepare ourselves to meet God, amen. We are seeing signs and wonders every turn we make. The devil is operating over time to destroy and steal the souls of Christians. We must stand strong on the *Word* of God, amen.

Reach out to one another in *love*, and let us encourage each other. Tremendous blessings today, in Jesus' name, amen. Shalom! Write a scripture on the line below, and for the day, share it with a friend today; tell them about Jesus and how they can be saved.

____

____

____

____

____

____

84

Thank God it's a new day, caregivers!

Life may not always be easy, but God is always good, amen. Let us hold on to Jesus Christ; He is the only way to the Father. Caregivers, Jesus said, "I am the way, the truth, and the life. No one can come to the Father except through me" (John 14:6, NLT). What do those words mean to you? When Jesus said these words, He was on the Earth teaching and preaching to His disciples before being betrayed and later crucified.

Jesus paid the price for all of our sins, amen. God the Father sent His only Son, Jesus, to bear all the sins of this world, so we all can live a life of abundance. Today without fear or worry, place all of your trust in Jesus Christ. Let us share a Jesus-kind of love with each other, amen. Today, take up your phone and call someone you have not spoken to for a while; tell them you love them in Jesus' name. Have a wonderful weekend with your family and friends. Always remember that Jesus Christ will always be Lord. Amen. Shalom!

____

____

____

____

____

____

85

Morning greetings, caregivers!

I want the entire world to know, "The Lord is my shepherd; I shall not want. He maketh me to lie down in green pastures: he leadeth me beside the still waters. He restoreth my soul: he leadeth me in the path of righteousness for his name's sake" (Psalm 23:1–3, KJV). Is God your shepherd? If not, would you consider making Him your Lord and Savior today? Today is our day of salvation. Let us take some time to examine ourselves, asking these questions:

Do I put God first in everything?

____

____

What aspect of my Christian life needs improvement?

____

____

____

____

____

____

Do you think God is pleased with your lifestyle?

____

What is the first thing you'll do today to fix your lifestyle in line with God's will?

Caregivers, our good Father is always watching and waiting on us. When we put God first, His blessings are in the overflow, amen. God woke us up this morning, so let's give Him all the praise and honor, in Jesus' name, amen. Shalom!

86

Happy morning to all caregivers!

The truth is Jesus Christ is our friend, our healer, our supply house, our councilor, and shalom. In reality, Jesus Christ is everything. So, whatever may be your situation, please take it to God in prayer, amen. Our day or night jobs may be long and tedious, but God will make them easy and short. All God asks of us is to trust Him. Trust God when your back is against the wall and there is no place to turn.

Caregivers, turn to Jesus Christ today and have faith because He is able to do the impossible; I can testify to that, amen. Whatever negative emotions we exhibit in the atmosphere, that's what the enemy wants. Be confident in the Lord Jesus Christ whom we serve, amen. May you be blessed, and you be a blessing to someone in Jesus' name, amen. Shalom!

____

____

____

____

____

____

87

Blessings to my caregivers!

Bible studies this morning for me focused on the gospel of John. The theological aspects of the resurrection of Jesus Christ. "Simon Peter said to them, 'I am going fishing.' They said to him, 'We will go with you'" (John 21:3, ESV). They went out and got into the boat, but that night they caught nothing. Returning the next morning, Peter and his fishermen had an encounter. It was the third time Jesus appeared after His resurrection, and He was not recognized.

Think about this point, Jesus is always with us, but we don't always recognize Him. I encourage everyone to read the entire gospels of Matthew, Mark, Luke, and John to understand the price that was paid for our sins. They all portray Jesus' life on Earth from a different perspective.

Caregivers, God sacrificed His only Son, Jesus, for us all. Food for thought, are we ready to make sacrifices for God? Beloved, let us start today; let us start to make sacrifices for God, amen. Let us join hands in unity and go fishing for souls, amen. God desires us to be good fishermen and women for Him. Stay blessed and focus on Jesus Christ, our only Savior, amen. Shalom!

88

Thank God, caregivers!

Let us give thanks unto God for keeping us safe and secure this week and always. "And out of them shall proceed thanksgiving and the voice of them that make merry and I will multiply them, and they shall not be few; I will also glorify them, and they shall not be small" (Jeremiah 30:19, KJV). God's promise is always true; we should open up our hearts and mouths, giving Him all the praise, honor, thanks, and glory. We sometimes take things for granted, not thinking about the source of our help.

Everything comes from God. He is our supply house, amen. Caregivers, we serve a great, wonderful, gigantic, loving, thoughtful, merciful, omnipresent, magnificent God. Trust God with your heart, and He will trust you with the keys to the kingdom of heaven. Be blessed and be a blessing to others in Jesus' name, amen. Shalom!

89

Good morning, caregivers!

"For God is good and His mercies endureth for ever" (Psalm 136, NIV).

Another day, in Jesus' name. Let us give thanks for God's grace, amen. What does it mean when we say, "God is good?" Do we use that line only when good things happen to us or when some terrible tragedy is avoided? Or is God still good when a loved one passes away or when things don't go our way? As human beings, sometimes we forget to thank God, whether good or bad.

First Thessalonians 5:18 (KJV) says, "In everything give thanks: for this is the will of God In Christ Jesus concerning you." The list of things to thank God for is without end, amen. Caregivers, let us always remember to thank God for everything. I, personally, am always in a thankful season, even when things might not be going the way I would like them to. From the moment my eyes are opened, I begin to thank and praise God.

There are so many people who went to bed and did not wake up. Caregivers, let us give thanks to God, our Abba Father, in Jesus' name today, amen. Shalom!

Even in this situation, God is still good:

90

Morning blessings to my caregivers!

"The Lord is my shepherd; I shall not want. He maketh me to lie down in green pastures: he leadeth me beside the still water…yea do I walk through the valley of the shadow of death, I will fear no evil: for thou art with me; thy rod and thy staff they comfort me" (Psalm 23, KJV). This is one of my favorite Psalms for many reasons. It is a source of comfort, knowing that God's promises are real and true. All that He promises, He fulfills.

I remember the time when I was homeless; God protected me. This is only one of the million downfalls I have experienced. Did I stay down? Absolutely not. The words of this Psalm kept me moving. I know I have someone who is taking good care of me. Today I can safely say, "The Lord is my shepherd," amen. Caregivers, today I want to encourage you to make Jesus Christ your shepherd. When we do, our blessing will be unlimited. Stay focused, stay blessed and meditate on the Word of God, in Jesus' name, amen. Shalom!

____

____

____

____

____

____

91

Good morning, caregivers!

Lord, You are Great!

Pleasant morning to all caregivers,

Each second of every minute of every hour of every day is the time to praise God, amen. Even when we are in the valley, God is great. A word of caution: when you are hanging on to God's Word, the enemy will work overtime to get your attention (be aware of this). Caregivers from today and beyond constantly praise God, thanking Him for everything. There is power in thanksgiving.

Today, let us pray.

Dear Jesus, I thank You. I, Lord, thank You for all the caregivers of this world.

May their daily walk with You be an everlasting blessing in Jesus' name, amen. Shalom!

Say your prayer:

____

____

____

____

____

____

92

Pleasant morning to my caregivers!

I greet each of you in the name of Jesus Christ. Lord, this morning, I lift up each caregiver and their household before You, in prayer, in Jesus' name. Jesus, bless them in every circumstance or situation in their lives, in Jesus' name. Never leave or forsake them in whatever they do. Whatever they may touch or want to achieve, grant it in Jesus' name. May prosperity overflow on their behalf in Jesus' name. Loosen all financial bondage and restore what the enemy and the cankerworms have stolen from them in Jesus' name. Make them live in the overflow of your heavenly blessings, in Jesus' name, amen.

Keep in prayerfulness, knowing that "The Lord is my light and my salvation; whom shall I fear? The Lord is the strength of my life, of whom shall I be afraid?" (Psalm 27:1, KJV) Caregivers, you can personalize scriptures and repeat them all the time. As a matter of fact, print them out on paper and place them on doors within your home, amen. In the time we are living in, we have to use the Word of God to defend and protect ourselves, amen. Stay in God's blessings this day and always in Jesus' name, amen. Shalom!

____

____

93

Blessed morning to all caregivers!

"I will praise thee with my whole heart: before the gods, I will sing praise unto thee" (Psalm 138:1, KJV). That's how we ought to approach our day with praise. Because of God's grace and mercy, we are still here, amen. Let us give a joyful shout-out to God, thanking Him for the breath in our lungs amongst the many other blessings. God is waiting to bless you today.

"And it shall come to pass, If thou shalt hearken diligently unto the voice of the Lord thy God, to observe and do all his commandments which I command thee this day, that the Lord thy God will set thee on high above all nations of the earth" (Deuteronomy 28:1, KJV).

God is ready to bless you right now, but all He asks of us is acknowledgment, amen. Caregivers, take the time out right this moment to say, "Thank You, Abba Father, who is in heaven." I trust that God will bless all caregivers today in Jesus' name, amen. Shalom!

____

____

____

____

94

Beautiful morning to all caregivers!

“This is the day which the Lord has made; we will rejoice and be glad in it” (Psalm 118:24, KJV). Are you truly happy in Jesus Christ? Do you spend unrushed quality time with Him? You can only find your true peace by meditating on God’s Word day and night. If the voices in your head are only on secular thoughts, there is no heavenly connection. It can only be changed by prayer and supplication to God.

Yes, I agree that things now have to be done in a timely fashion, but we need to make time for God, amen. The second coming of our Lord and Savior, Jesus Christ, is about to take place. Ever ask yourself, “If I went to bed and did not wake up one morning, where would I spend eternity?”

Let us prepare to meet God; I want all caregivers to be in the number that John saw in *Revelation*, amen. We must be singing and praising our way to heaven. No one knows of that day Jesus is coming, so prepare, amen. I bring these encouraging words in Jesus’ name, amen. Shalom!

____

____

____

95

Glorious morning to all caregivers!

> But when the morning came, Jesus stood on the shore: but the disciples knew not that it was Jesus. Then Jesus saith unto them, Children, have ye any meat? They answer him, No. And then he said unto them, Cast the net on the right side of the ship, and ye shall find.

John 21:4–6a (KJV)

Caregivers, this was after Jesus Christ was resurrected, His third appearance. Seven of His disciples went out to fish that night but returned the next morning empty-handed. Close to the shore in the boat, they could not see who was asking them if they had caught any fish. They answered anyhow, a good example to us all to be always obedient to what God asks of us.

The disciples obeyed even if they could not identify who the speaker was, amen. It's called having faith. We are called to serve in the kingdom of heaven. When the disciples followed the very specific instructions they were given, they were rewarded with fish in abundance, amen. Starting today, let us be obedient to God and reap the unlimited abundance of blessings.

Today, Lord Jesus, I prayed for an abundance of blessings upon each caregiver in Jesus' name, amen. Shalom!

____

____

____

____

____

____

96

Good morning, caregivers!

When we worship God, we are inviting God's presence in our hearts.

Praise and worship are a very important part of oneness with God. Do you worship God from the sincereness of your hearts? Or just go through the formality, mumbling a few words during the commute or in the shower, just to tell yourself you prayed. Set aside quality time in the presence of the Lord, read your *Bible*, amen.

Caregivers, miracles do happen when we honor God with our prayers and thanksgiving. Today, I want to encourage everyone to spend time with God. Talk to Him, tell Him how much you love Him; God wants to hear from you today. Because of God's love, we can do all things. Have a fruitful and Blessed day in Jesus' name, amen. Shalom!

____

____

____

____

____

____

97

Caregivers, thank God!

Let us pray:

Dear Jesus,

Thank You for keeping all the caregivers. Abba Father, guide and protect each of them in Jesus' name. Grant them everlasting mercies and grace. Protect them and their loved ones from the seen and unseen evil that is lurking about in Jesus' name. May everything that they endeavor to do or touch prosper in Jesus' name, amen.

We must always keep a positive attitude in life. At times you may feel that you have more than you can tolerate, but Philippians 2:13 (KJV) says, "I can do all things through Christ which strengthens me." Today, don't matter what comes your way; keep on pressing on in Jesus' name, amen. Shalom!

____

____

____

____

____

____

98

Happy morning to all caregivers!

"This is the confidence we have in approaching God: that if we ask anything according to his will, he hears us" (1 John 5:14, NIV). In today's world, we find people who place their confidence in their position, finance, authority, or friends. As children of God, where should our confidence be placed? Without a doubt, our confidence should be in God, amen. God hears us at all times, so there is nothing to worry about; God always listens.

I always believe God created all the animals in the forest, birds in the air, and fish in the ocean, and they are well taken care of. God holds the original plan for everyone and everything. It brings comfort to us as Christians, knowing that God has a plan for each of us. Caregivers, continue walking in obedience to God's true purpose.

Praise the Lord. Caregivers, trust in God, our Lord and Savior, with confidence, amen.

Have a wonderful day in Jesus' name, amen. Shalom!

____

____

____

____

____

____

99

Dear Jesus, thank You for all caregivers!

Morning blessings. I was doing interesting research recently. It was in relation to the women disciples who followed Jesus when He walked the Earth. What was most interesting, they were never mentioned much in the Gospels. It makes sense to me as to who did the cleaning, washing, cooking, and the like. My discovery also clarified that there *actually were* women disciples. My point is, women are very important in the kingdom of God. Let us consider our worth and stand proud and tall.

Throughout the scriptures from the first woman Eve, Mary, mother of Jesus, Ruth the Moabite, Mary Magdalene, Rachel, Hannah, Deborah, Ester, Miriam, Sarah, Elizabeth, Priscilla, Mary of Bethany, Martha, Jehosheba, and us, female caregivers. We all represent greatness.

As women, we have an integral part to play in God's kingdom business. Therefore, let us rededicate ourselves to the task of discipleship on Earth. Consider your worth moving forward, and take your rightful places. God wants us to live in the abundance of His blessings. Starting from today, right now, claim your status in Jesus' name, amen. Shalom! What is the gift God has given to as a woman of God:

100

Pleasant good morning to all caregivers!

In everything, Lord, we give *You* thanks.

Psalm 136:1 (KJV) says, "O give thanks unto the Lord; for he is good: for his mercy endureth forever." Caregivers, at all times, we should be in a thanksgiving mood, amen. The unlimited favors God has bestowed upon us are reasons enough.

Let us pray:

Abba Father,

I thank You for the breath in my lungs. I thank You for waking me up this morning and giving me another opportunity to say, "Thank You." In Jesus' name, amen.

Caregivers, don't allow any distraction from the devil to take you away from the things of God. For the many who are in search of employment, don't be discouraged; God is making way for you in Jesus' name. I will keep in prayers always in Jesus' mighty name, amen. Shalom!

____

____

____

____

____

101

Greetings, caregivers, in the mighty name of Jesus Christ!

"Fear thou not; for I am with thee: be not dismayed; for I am thy God: I will strengthen thee, I will help thee; yea, I will uphold thee with the right hand of my righteousness" (Isaiah 41:10, KJV). Are you living in fear? Today is your day to let go *of all* the fears in your life. These are some of the things that make us fearful: finance, health, family, employment, death, sickness, and more. You have all right to be concerned, but knowing and believing all that God promises should wipe away all of the fears.

I could share with you from my personal life experiences how I learned to trust in God without a doubt. When life challenges hit me, I stand on the *Word* of God; when sickness attacks my family—I fight back with scripture, "By *His* [Jesus] stripes we are healed" (Isaiah 53:5, NKJV). (Hereinafter, emphasis added.) When death comes, I grieve in God's comforting embrace, "The Lord is close to the brokenhearted, and saveth those who are crushed in spirit" (Psalm 34:18, NIV).

For every situation you face, there is comfort in God's Word. Caregivers, place all your trust in God today, and *He* will trust you with the keys to the kingdom of heaven, amen. Be blessed in Jesus' name, amen. Shalom!

102

Thank You, Jesus, for caregivers!

Prepare us, Lord, for the coming of thy heavenly kingdom. May God bless and keep each of you in Jesus' name. "He who dwells in the shelter of the most high will abide in the shadow of the Almighty" (Psalm 91:1, ESV). God is our protector, our supplier, our healer; He is our everything, amen. You may be dealing with a desperate situation; take it to God in prayer, and consider it done, hallelujah.

As believers, you must stand on the *Word* of God. Believing without a doubt that He is more than able to solve all your problems, amen. The days of favors are about to open up in your life. "So faith comes by hearing and hearing by the *word* of Christ" (Romans 10:17, ESV). We serve a faithful, loving God. Caregivers, be encouraged that God is in control. May you and your household be blessed in Jesus' name, amen. Shalom! What are you trusting God with today:

____

____

____

____

____

____

103

Blessed morning!

Greetings to all caregivers!

I remember as a child growing up hearing my mom crying out to God when there was nothing for us children to eat. The flour to bake is done, so is the rice, etc. Praise the Lord; her earnest prayers work. God doesn't ever get tired of hearing the same request over and over; He is not like mankind, who would probably murmur beneath the breath, saying, "Again," in frustration.

So continue talking to your Heavenly Father, telling Him how much you love and appreciate Him, and laying all your petitions before His throne, amen. God's love for everyone is unconditional and limitless. Caregivers practice spending quality time in the presence of God, praying and studying His Word.

The more you study your Bible, the more you will be able to apply it to your life for rewarding results. "So then faith cometh by hearing, and hearing by the word of God" (Romans 10:17, KJV). There is power in the name of Jesus; stay fruitful and faithful in Jesus' name, amen. Shalom!

104

Morning blessings to all of my caregivers!

I greet each of you in no other name but the name of Jesus Christ. Question: Are you being fruitful in your spiritual walk with God? The Bible teaches us that Jesus destroyed a fig tree because of barrenness. It was a fig tree covered with green leaves and should have had figs on it (Matthew 3:8–10, 7:16–20, 13:8; Luke 3:7–9).

The fig tree represents Christians or the church ministry as a body. They run around putting on an outward show, but on closer examination, their spiritual roots are withering or dried up. Let us examine ourselves today, looking for areas that need spiritual nutrients or revival, amen. Caregivers, God wants us to be fruitful and prosperous in every area of our lives. Let us be good ambassadors for the kingdom of heaven. Daily disciples, we ought to be, telling others about Jesus.

Let us pray:

Dear Jesus, today, I pray over every area in a caregiver's life. I asked that You, Lord, refresh them anewб physically and spiritually. In Jesus' name, amen. Shalom!

105

Glorious morning, caregivers!

I trust that the week is going great so far, in Jesus' name. Caregivers, God wants to take care of you in every possible way. "Be careful for nothing; but in everything by prayer and supplication with thanksgiving let your requests be known unto God. And the peace of God which passeth all understanding; shall keep your hearts and minds through Christ Jesus" (Philippians 4:6–7, KJV). It is all up to you to choose; eternal happiness in Jesus Christ or a miserable life with the devil.

God loves each and every one of us unconditionally. My encouragement today is don't ever give up; you may be waiting for a breakthrough; it is about to happen in Jesus' name. Stay focused on God and the things of His kingdom. God is about to bless you tremendously, have a wonderful day in Jesus' name, amen. Shalom!

____

____

____

____

____

____

106

Good morning, caregivers!

This is the Lord's day; let us give Him a great big shout; thank You, Jesus! Caregivers, God has been and will continue to keep us, amen. His mercies and grace are limitless. It is a great day in the Lord. Every day that we are given another opportunity is enough to be thankful for. May God bless and keep all of you. May all your dreams come through in Jesus' name. "This is the day which the Lord has made. We will rejoice and be glad in it" (Psalm 118:24, NLT). Jesus loves you, amen. Shalom!

____

____

____

____

____

____

107

Good morning, caregivers!

I look up at a note pin on my computer screen. It says: God loves you. I immediately felt the presence of the Lord; He was putting His arms around me, and I felt loved. Happy morning, my caregivers; I want to let you know that God loves you, amen. It is contagious; share His love today. Throughout the Scripture, we see God expressing His love for the world. From the sacrificing of His Son Jesus to the rainbow, He dresses in the sky, keeping His promises of love and grace. Love one another with the love of God, amen. Have a wonderful day in Jesus' name, amen. Shalom!

____

____

____

____

____

____

108

Good morning, caregivers!

Always remember you are not alone. We serve a God who comforts us. "And when I saw him, I fell at His feet as dead. And He laid His right hand upon me, saying unto me, Fear not; I am the first and the last…" (Revelation 1:17, KJV) Caregivers, have no fear; Jesus Christ is our comforter, amen. This is a good moment; this is the time to say, "Thank You, Lord, for comforting me when I was down and out." When the doctors had given up on me, God did not.

Receive your breakthroughs in Jesus' name. When my marriage was on the rocks, God fixed it. When my children chose not to listen, God brought them back to the fold. We can go on and on with the many instances God has saved us. List some of yours:

____

____

____

____

____

____

And He will continue to carry us when we cannot carry ourselves, amen. God's promises are always yes, and amen. "Jesus said unto him, I am the way, the truth, and the life: no man cometh unto the Father, but by me" (John 14:6, KJV). Open your hearts today and allow Jesus Christ to take complete control. Your life is not going to be the same. You are going to experience true happiness in the comfort of God our Father. Have a wonderful day in Jesus' mighty name, amen. Shalom!

109

Good morning, caregivers!

We are our neighbor's keeper! "Thou shalt not avenge, nor bear any grudge against the children of thy people, but thou shalt love thy neighbor as thyself: I am the Lord" (Leviticus 19:18, KJV). How difficult it feels when someone hurts you terribly to forgive them. Or when someone tells an untruth about you. We immediately stop all conversations and want no further interaction with that individual. But that is not how God expects us to be; we were made in the image and likeness of God. Then our behavior should portray godly behavior. "And be ye kind one to another, tenderhearted, forgiving one another, even as God for Christ's sake hath forgiven you" (Ephesians 4:32, KJV).

In times like these, there is no room for animosity or ill feelings to one another. This is what Jesus said to His disciple: "Then came Peter to him, and said, Lord, how often does my brother sin against me, and I forgive him? till seven times? Jesus said unto him, I say not unto thee, Until seven times: but, Until seventy times seven" (Matthew 18:21–22, KJV). Let us examine ourselves today and think about that brother or sister that needs to be forgiven. Write his/her name here: ______________________________

_______________.

Pray to God to give you a heart of forgiveness in order

for you to be forgiven. I remember a time in my life when a past husband left with everything we had earned, including the money in the bank. I was left with all the bills and an eviction notice. I had to sleep on a futon bed. Yes, I was hurt. I cried and cried, wondering how I would manage. But God stepped in and began a good work in me, amen. I did not lose my mind; I did not commit suicide but held on to Jesus. That's when I truly discovered that God loves me.

My healing, physically and mentally, began a few years later when I finally confronted him. I just suddenly said, "I forgive you"; he was surprised. Then I said it louder, "I forgive you." His words were, "I kept on thinking I don't want to die knowing what I had done to you was so wrong." After that day, our Abba Father went to work in my life; everything and more was restored, hallelujah.

Caregivers, reach out to that person who may have hurt you in some way or the other, tell them that you forgive them; it is not that hard to do; unburden yourself. God is about to bless you in a mighty way. Lord Jesus, forgive us so that we can forgive others in Jesus' name, amen. Shalom!

____

____

____

____

____

____

110

Having confidence in God!

You may be in need of a breakthrough or many breakthroughs and don't know what to do or where to turn this morning. "Let us, therefore, come boldly unto the throne of grace to help in time of need" (Hebrews 4:16, KJV). I am here to encourage you today; please turn to Jesus Christ, amen. Each morning while I am getting dressed, I listen to a Christian broadcast called *Fixing the Money Thing*. I was especially drawn to today's message. The pastor was teaching about allowing God to bless us.

I immediately began to reflect on the many times in my life I had to run around chasing money. I was working two and three jobs, but still, the money was not enough. It was not until I learned how to exercise my faith in Jesus Christ I began to see breakthroughs. The bills and everything else still come, I am currently working one job, but all my bills are paid with excess to save by God. Caregivers, this is a hallelujah moment. I can stand boldly and shout, "Jesus Christ of Nazareth, pay my bills and still leave extra to save!" Amen.

Today let us walk in confidence, "So that we may boldly say, The Lord is my helper, and I will not fear what man shall do unto me" (Hebrews 13:6, KJV). As Christians, we have to stand on the Word of God. It is called "exercising your faith." I pray that all caregivers will receive this blessing in Jesus' name, amen. Shalom!

____

____

____

____

____

____

111

Good morning, caregivers!

It's only the blood of Jesus that was shed on Calvary that can make us whole again. It affirms what the scripture says, Jesus Christ already paid the price for caregivers; all of our sins, shame, guilt, and shortcomings were left at the cross of Calvary, amen. "Come now, and let us reason together, saith the Lord: though your sins be as scarlet, they shall be as white as snow; though they be red like crimson, they shall be as wool" (Isaiah 1:18, KJV).

No one is exempt from the kingdom of God; He welcomes all who choose Him. You may be thinking right now that there is no hope for you. I am here to let you know that there is always hope in Jesus Christ. Go before God, humble yourself, confess *all* your wrongdoings, and ask God for His forgiveness. Ask Him to "Create in me a clean heart, O God; and renew a right spirit within me" (Psalm 51:10, KJV). Don't walk around carrying the burdens of guilt and shame anymore; Jesus is waiting.

A hug makes you feel loved, protected, safe, not alone, and secure. With arms wide open, Jesus is waiting. Jesus, this morning, I pray for everyone who is reading this message. Lord, touch them in tremendous ways. Keep and protect them and their loved ones, in Jesus' name, amen, Shalom!

112

Good morning, caregivers!

Let us give thanks to God for today; God is good and merciful, amen. God's love is everlasting and sure. As you begin this work day, may God pour out showers of blessing upon you and your family in Jesus' name.

Let us pray.

Dear Jesus,

I look to You, Lord. Even when it feels like all hope is gone, I will continue to look to You. You are my healer, my provider, my comforter, my everything. I will always put You first, in Jesus' name, amen. For those in search of a job, receive it right now in Jesus' name. Stay focused and faithful in Jesus almighty God's name, amen. Shalom!

Say your prayer:

____

____

____

____

____

____

113

Good morning, caregivers!

What is faith? Romans 10:17 (NKJV) tells us, "So then faith cometh by hearing, and hearing by the word of God." I am sure many of us can give many great examples of faith-filled experiences. The frequent times when there were no groceries or food to cook for the kids. Or the time when unemployment hits so hard, just when you think it cannot get any worse, a spouse dies. But you kept on praying and trusting God until that relief came.

Caregivers, this is called having "faith." I recall that one year when everything was just going wrong. My one-and-a-half-year-old son was under serious attack, asthma, bronchitis, pneumonia, allergies, and high fever. I looked at his frail body in the hospital bed, praying and trusting God for a miracle. I could not work; I had lost the shelter over our heads, so homelessness crept in.

Many days I wanted to give up, but I did not. At that time, I was standing in faith in Jesus Christ for healing and restoration, and to my delight, God heard my prayers and granted me my reward; He saved my son. He saved us. How many of us today are going through situations and think it cannot get any worse? I am here to let you know that to keep on having faith in God for your miracle, amen.

Always remember, “Faith is the substance of things hoped for, the evidence of things not seen” (Hebrews 11:1, KJV). It is already done; your miracles have already taken place. Receive it today in Jesus’ name, amen. Shalom!

____

____

____

____

____

____

114

Standing on the Word of God!

> To everything, there is a season and a time to every purpose under heaven. A time to be born, and a time to die; a time to plant, and a time to pluck up that which is planted. A time to kill, and a time to heal; a time to break down, and time to build up; A time to weep, and a time to laugh; a time to mourn, and a time to dance; A time to cast away stones, and a time to gather stones together; A time to embrace, and a time to cease from embracing; A time to get, and a time to lose; A time to keep, and a time to cast away; A time to rend, and a time to sew; A time to keep silence, and a time to speak; A time to love, and a time to hate; A time of war, and a time of peace.

Ecclesiastes 3:1–8 (KJV)

Caregivers, for everything in your life, there is a season. You may go through a season of sickness, anger, financial hardship, unemployment, family upheaval, confusion, loss of a loved one, and child or children disobedience. But it would not last forever. We serve a God of love who would see us through. All He asked of us is to make Him, Lord and Savior, in and of our lives. Put God first in everything that you do.

These are His words, "Ask, and it shall be given you, seek, and ye shall find; knock, and it shall be open unto you: for every one that asketh receives; and he that seeketh findeth, and to him that knocketh it shall be opened" (Matthew 7:7–8, KJV). Let us all go before God today in prayer and supplication for unlimited favors and breakthroughs, in Jesus' name, amen. Shalom!

____

____

____

____

____

____

115

Are we living the way God wants us to live financially? For some of us, absolutely *not*!

God knew you before you were born. As we grow older, we tend to come into our understanding. Doing what we want, regardless. Especially after the age of eighteen, we follow the lies of the devil, who uses the world systems to tell us it's okay to accept all the lines of credit cards. The credit card system was designed to trap us in debt. It is easy to pull out a card and run up bills. Before you realize it, you are thousands of dollars in debt. When you cannot pay, the collectors will ceaselessly call.

Caregivers, before you get there, if you have not reached it yet, pull your breaks. Seek the kingdom of God to direct your life pertaining to your finances. The scripture clearly states, "But seek ye first the kingdom of God, and his righteousness, and all these things shall be added unto you" (Matthew 6:33, KJV). For financial directions, study, write down, dissect, and understand the law that governs the kingdom of God, specifically in the areas of your finance. For too long, we have been trapped in believing the wrong thing. God wants you to prosper in the overflow, amen.

Set goals to live below your income level, set goals for your savings, and stop impulsive buying. Getting rid of all credit cards is a huge step in the right direction. Lastly, don't forget to *give*. I have seen what giving back can accomplish. Luke 6:38 (NIV) says, "Give, and it will be given unto you; good measure, pressed down, and shaken together running over."

Every time we give, we are declaring that we are blessed, obedient, and righteous. There are many more scriptures to help you in your studies on finance in God's way. Lord, I pray that Your people will take You, Father, at Your Word for financial freedom in Jesus' mighty name, men. Shalom! What scripture did you study that can help you manage your finances well?

____

____

____

____

____

____

116

Good morning, caregivers!

Thank You, Jesus, for keeping us safe throughout this week. Thank You, Lord, for providing for us. Father, thank You for Your mercies and grace. Thank You for loving us in Jesus' name. Amen.

Caregivers, keep your eyes on Jesus Christ. He is our commander in chief, He is our *Elohim*, He is our redeemer, and He is our Heavenly Father who loves us unconditionally. There is confidence in knowing without a doubt that only God can do for us what He says. I want to encourage you today, don't matter what comes your way, hold on to Jesus. You may not see the results you want when you want, but it's all in God's time.

"Be careful for nothing; but in everything by prayer and supplication with thanksgiving let your requests be made known unto God" (Philippians 4:6, KJV). You don't have to convince God of anything, just be in continuous prayer. Prayer opens the doors to impossible possibilities. Have a wonderful day and weekend with your family. Stay safe in Jesus' name, amen. Shalom!

____

____

117

We are our brother's keeper, amen. God wants us to love one another with our whole hearts. According to God's Word, "Be kindly affectionate one to another with brotherly love; in honor preferring one another…" (Matthew 12:10, KJV) Today, in Jesus' name, we are going to lift up our brothers and sisters in countries, where the people are subdued and under siege in prayer.

People are suffering and dying and are in dire need of a miracle from God. Agreement in prayer moves the hands of God, amen.

Heavenly Father,

This morning, we stand in agreement to break the bonds of strife and siege that are plaguing the countries of this world. You said it in Your Word, "For where two or three are gathered together in my name, there am I in the midst of them" (Matthew 18:20, KJV).

Lord, we pray for Your divine intervention wherever it is needed in Jesus' name. The alarming number of Your people are suffering and dying daily. Lord, only You can stop the chaos in Jesus' name.

As we stand before You in agreement, Lord, we are standing on Your Word, "If my people who are called by my name, would humble themselves pray and seek my face and turn from their wicked way, then I will hear from heaven and will forgive their sins, and will heal this land" (2 Chronicles 7:14, KJV).

This morning, Jesus, as we pray, we are pleading the blood of Jesus for forgiveness and healing. Innocent men, women, and children are dying at the hands of wicked men. Lord, have mercy upon Your children. Harden not Your heart, Lord, against them; remember them all in Your mercies. Mankind has sinned and come short many times, but You said, "[...] a broken and contrite heart you will not despise" (Psalm 51:17, KJV).

We thank You, Lord, for the atmospheric shift that is happening right now in Jesus' name. We give You, Abba, all the praise and honor in Jesus' name, amen. Shalom!

N.B.: Feel free to add to this prayer as the Spirit leads:

____

____

____

____

____

____

118

Be thankful for today!

The word "tomorrow" is the day after today. Is tomorrow yours? Is tomorrow mine?

It is said, "To day if ye hear his voice, harden not your hearts…" (Hebrews 3:15, KJV)

Some of us live with great expectations of seeing another day; for others, they think tomorrow is guaranteed. How about changing that mindset? Tomorrow is not promised or guaranteed. Only God knows what tomorrow will bring and if it will at all. So in every second, minute, or hour as we possibly can, let us be thankful and very grateful for today.

So many of us go to bed with a to-do list, thinking tomorrow I would do this and that, but either tomorrow never came or tomorrow met them in the bed of affliction. Years ago, I read a book called *Power of Now* by Eckhart Tolle. It confirmed my thoughts on many levels. If we don't let go of the past, it creates a problem. If we worry about the future, we have no control. All we have is right now.

Today is the day to serve the true and living God. Today is the day to pick up your phone and reach out to say, "I am sorry." The list can go on and on. Please don't wait until tomorrow. Today is the day to pray and ask God for forgiveness. As my late granny used to say, "Today is the day of salvation." Accept Jesus Christ as your Lord and Savior today; tomorrow may be too late. I trust that someone may be encouraged; God is waiting on you today. Have a wonderful day *today* in Jesus' name, amen. Shalom!

____

____

____

____

____

____

119

Good morning, caregivers!

Are we followers of man or of God? God created mankind in his image. The Bible contains the answers to life's many questions. But to gain those answers, we should be followers of God.

> It is your God you must follow, and him you must revere. Keep his commandments and obey him; serve him and hold fast to him […] The Lord himself goes before you and will be with you; he will never leave you nor forsake you, do not be afraid; or discouraged.
>
> Deuteronomy 13:4; 31:8 (NIV)

All these are God's true promises.

"Then spake Jesus again unto them, saying. I am the light of the world: he that followeth me shall not walk in darkness, but shall have the light of life" (John 8:12, KJV). For many Christians, reading and correctly understanding the Word of God may be a bit of a challenge. But don't be afraid; here is where the Holy Spirit comes in. Remember, we serve the triune God—Father, Son, and Holy Spirit—

all three are *one*.

Caregivers, as we study God's Word, pray and ask for wisdom and understanding. Moreover, it is important to educate yourself by reading and studying your Bible daily. Find authentic, credible sources to help with the interpretation of God's Word. Don't be deceived by untrustworthy search engines. Let God be your guide, "So then faith cometh by hearing, and hearing by the Word of God" (Romans 10:17, KJV). I pray that these few words encourage you today to seek and follow God. Have a truly great day in Jesus' name, amen. Shalom!

____

____

____

____

____

____

120

If tomorrow never comes, are we prepared to meet God? We wake up daily and rush to get to our jobs. Work hard all day, rush home tired, sometimes nodding off. Eventually, getting into bed, tossing and turning in an exhausted sleep. Waking the next morning to start the same routine all over again. Did you make time to pray, to thank God for waking you up to live another day?

In today's life of hustle and bustle, please set aside time for God. Any one of us can go to bed and never wake up. I make it a habit each night before going to bed to hold my husband's hand and thank God for the day, for His protection, for His provisions, for His healing, for His favor, for everything. I would like to encourage you, caregivers, please remember your maker before it is too late. Jesus' love for you is like no other. If tomorrow never comes, we will be with God in heaven. Have a wonderful day, in Jesus' name, amen. Shalom!

____

____

____

____

____

____

121

Having faith in God!

Many times, we strive hard on our own, trying to get things done. While forgetting it is not solely up to us. God is the Alpha and Omega of everything. We cannot do anything on our own. I suggest today to place everything in the hands of Jesus Christ. Never second guess what God can do; believe and you shall receive.

"[…] a certain man lame from his mother's womb was carried, whom they laid daily at the gate of the temple which is called Beautiful" (Acts 3:2, KJV). This man was placed there strategically daily to beg, but the disciples saw something in this man. He could have stayed home and fretted and complained because he could not walk. Yet when Peter told him to look at them, and Peter took his hand to stand, by his faith that he could stand, he did.

Due to his obedience and belief, he received healing in Jesus' name. That's the kind of faith I am talking about. Your cupboard may be empty, but God is going to fill it. Your body may be sick but walk around praising God. Receive all your blessings in Jesus' name. Caregivers, no matter what you are going through today, have faith that God will make it right in Jesus' name, amen. Shalom!

122

God has a plan for your life!

Sometimes in life, God allows things to happen. At that moment, we may ask, "Why, Lord? Why did You let my loved one die? Why is my family always broke? Why can't I find a job? Why is my job so difficult? Why am I homeless?" Why, why, why. But don't lose heart; God has not forgotten you. He has major plans for your life. "For I know the thoughts that I think toward you, saith the Lord, thoughts of peace, and not of evil, to give you an expected end" (Jeremiah 29:11, KJV).

I remember holding my dead child for the first and last time, asking God, "Why?" Years later, I got my answer. I felt good knowing that she was with God, and one day we were going to be reunited. Just as God had used the prophet Jeremiah to deliver the good news to suffering people years ago, He is doing the same for me today. Quit the questioning and complaining. God is not on the same level as mankind. His promises are always kept for the right time. "For no matter how many promises God has made, they are always 'Yes' in Christ. And through him, the 'Amen' is spoken by us to the glory of God" (2 Corinthians 1:20, NIV). Stay courageous; God has a master plan for our lives. Be blessed in Jesus' name, amen. Shalom!

How do you help others through your suffering and loss?

____

____

____

____

____

____

123

God is always with you!

Ever had those moments when nothing is going right, and you feel all alone? One time or another, it happens, but you are not alone. Above all those who claim to love you, the best lover of all is Jesus Christ. He is the best security guard of all, best healer of all, and best friend of all. Even when we don't feel God's presence, He is there walking with us, protecting us from harm.

Caregivers, please take some time today to acknowledge God, your eternal Father. Listening while walking with God is essential; make time for God because He always makes time for you. God is always with us; it doesn't matter where we are. Stay blessed in Jesus' name, amen. Shalom!

____

____

____

____

____

____

Meme

Meme is an undocumented worker who migrated to America from Brazil on a tourist visa and decided to stay. When she packed her two pieces of luggage and left Brazil, she was leaving a lot of hurt and pain behind. Both of her parents died in a tragic car accident. She was raised by her aunt and her aunt's husband. Between the age of five to fifteen, she was raped and molested by her aunt's husband. Every time she would tell her aunt, she would be called a liar and beaten mercilessly. At fifteen years, unable to tolerate it and pregnant, she ran away. Meme quickly found herself in a relationship with an older man who promised to look after her. That did not last long before he started to abuse her. Seven months pregnant and bleeding, she was pushed out of a speeding car by her supposed boyfriend and left for dead on the side of the road.

Unconscious and badly damaged, she was found by an old farmer on his way to his garden. He quickly got some help and took her back to his humble home. Even though her unborn child was killed, her life was saved. She spent the next ten years living in this village. She learned about God and His goodness and love. When the opportunity came to apply for a visa to America, she took it and got through. With butterflies in her stomach, she believed that God was going to take care of her. She told me that she has a deep yearning to know about God in her heart. She explained it like this: "Even though hiding in America is living in plain sight." Her life in America is much better than the one she had in Brazil. She worked throughout the pandemic and survived, to God be the glory.

124

Good morning, caregivers!

Standing strong as Christians.

"In the last days there will be difficult times. For people will only love themselves and their money. They will be boastful and proud, scoffing at God, […]. They will be unloving and unforgiving…" (2 Timothy 3:1–9, NLT) Caregivers, Paul was writing about what to expect in the last days. Are we experiencing some or all of what was written many years ago? Yes, we are seeing the signs of the approach of Jesus' second coming.

However, while we see the signs, we must not be wowed by them and so consumed that we lose focus of God and furthering His kingdom. During these times, be watchful and prayerful. Jesus' Word says:

> Don't let anyone mislead you, for many will come in my name, claiming, "I am the Messiah," and saying the time has come! But don't believe them. And when you hear of wars and insurrection, don't panic. Yes, these things must take place first, but the end won't follow immediately…
>
> Luke 21:5–12 (NLT)

Let us prepare ourselves; there are more to come. But

the good news is God is our protector, amen. I am not trying to scare anyone, just making sure each of you makes it to heaven with me. Please read the entire chapter in your Bible and believe that Jesus can save you to be with Him at the end. Have a great day with family and friends in Jesus' name, amen. Shalom!

____

____

____

____

____

____

125

Having the godly type of faith!

What is faith? "Faith shows the reality of what we hope for; it is the evidence of things we cannot see" (Hebrews 11:1, NLT). As believers, we know that faith moves the hands of God. You can read and study the entire chapter within the Bible on faith. Numbers went on to give great examples of faith, how it worked in ancient times and how we can apply it today.

You may be trusting God for situation breakthroughs, whether it is healing, a spouse, or financial security, and although it seems like forever and impossible, you must believe God is working on your behalf and stand on your faith in Jesus. Your blessings are about to take place in Jesus' name. Your "Boaz" is about to put in his appearance. Your bank account is about to overflow in Jesus' name. Your children are about to come back home in Jesus' name.

I implore you, however, not to expect *God* to give you exactly what you ask for all the time. Sometimes you ask for the winning lottery numbers, and *God* opens up a job opportunity for you because He knows winning the lottery will pollute and destroy you, but this job will open doors to further wealth. Be weary not to shun *God's blessing*s because of the package it comes in or because it is not exact.

Whatever your needs are this morning, *God* is more than able to meet them. Hallelujah! Let us continue praying and trusting God for everything in Jesus' name you will receive. Amen. Shalom!

____

____

____

____

____

____

126

Good morning, caregivers!

Let us pray:

Lord Jesus, Ruler of the universe. This morning, I boldly come before Your throne.

I am praying to You, Lord, on behalf of all the caregivers who are reading this right now in Jesus' name. Jesus, bless them and their family in tremendous ways. Bring out the leadership and creative skills in each of them in Jesus' name. Thank You, Jesus, for Your love, thank You for Your grace, thank You for providing, thank You for healing, thank You for the breath in our lungs.

Jesus, Your promise for all of us is to live in the overflow of Your blessings.

Mighty God, keep us under Your grace. Grant us more and more wisdom in Jesus' mighty name, amen.

Caregivers, feel free to personalize this little prayer, adding or subtracting as you desire.

____

____

____

____

In times like these, we need God; we need a Savior. Praying to God is not difficult. At times we may hear others pray and desire to pray like him or her. Praying is talking to God, in thanksgiving, simply from your heart. Psalm 51:17 (NIV) says, "My sacrifice, O God, is a broken spirit; a broken and contrite heart you, God, will not despise." Stay in God's Word, and have a truly wonderful day in Jesus' name, amen. Shalom!

127

Ignoring the devil

"Look, I have given you authority over all the power of the enemy, and you can walk among snakes and scorpions and crush them. Nothing will injure you" (Luke 10:19, NLT). God's Word is true to those who believe. Today, my encouragement is don't waste precious time on the devil; he was defeated years ago.

I once knew a man who was obsessed with the devil, every word that came out of his mouth daily was about evil people doing this or that to him or his family. One day he wore a pair of very tight shoes and eventually got two blisters on his big toes. His big toes got inflamed, and both nails fell off. He eventually went to see a false prophet, who told him that his neighbor did something to his feet to hurt or maim him. The end was horrible.

Firstly, it cost him thousands of dollars just to get advice from the false prophet. Next, the mixture of things he was given caused all the toenails to get inflamed, and they fell off. As a result, he ended up in the hospital with a serious infection. A few of his toes had to be removed because of gangrene. This narrative describes how the devil operates. He comes to defeat and conquer, bringing suspicious thoughts and ideas to distract and destroy you.

Caregivers, don't waste your time on the enemy; let God fight your battles. The Bible so rightly says, "So humble yourself before God. Resist the devil, and he will flee from you" (James 4:7, NLT). In a nutshell, as Christians, we should put on the whole armor of God. Ephesians 6:10–20 describe what God's armor is. But don't be confused; the Bible also warned about spiritual wickedness in high places and to have discernment, as in 1 Corinthians 12:10 (NLT). The devil is defeated. When the negative attacks come, pray about it and move on, "[…] Get thee behind me, Satan…" (Luke 4:8, KJV) Don't allow the spirit of fear to conquer you. Stay strong in prayer in Jesus' name, amen. Shalom!

____

____

____

____

____

____

128

Being a good servant!

How do we develop a servanthood heart? Caregivers, here are a few steps that could help you accomplish that.

First, by being humble, when you submit yourself to God, He lifts you up. An example: We all know that, at times, work can be difficult, but instead of complaining, take it to God in prayer. Your day will end, and you will not feel overwhelmed anymore. God will even reward you with a better job or a better situation. God works in mighty and mysterious ways. Daily, we must live doing humble service for others.

Second, Jesus served His disciples by washing the feet of His disciples, amongst other kind deeds. If you see a need, please don't hesitate and serve by example. Jesus Christ is the greatest servant of all servants. As Christians, it is important to serve others. Reach out to the seniors and sick people around you to ask them how you can be of help. Call that sister who is not working, and ask her what she needs. These are only some of the ways we can be good servants while doing the work of God, amen. Shalom!

____

____

____

____

129

Confidence in God

Today, I will address a very deep concern. Marriage and family. I am moved by what is happening daily. Men and women are allowing the enemy to win. The devil is on his agenda to steal and destroy families. For too long, we ignore what God's Word says about marriage; it was started first by God. "And the LORD God said, 'It is not good that the man should be alone; I shall make him a helper suitable for him" (Genesis 2:18, NIV).

After God made the first bride and groom, He blessed them and sent them out to copulate, multiply and rule the Earth. "Therefore shall a man leave his father and mother, and shall cleave unto his wife: and they shall be one flesh" (Genesis 2:34, ESV). But today, what do we see happening? Total disobedience to God. "Marriage is honorable in all, and the bed is undefiled: but whoremongers and adulterers God will judge…" (Hebrews 13:4, ESV)

"Husbands, love your wives, even as Christ loved the church, and gave himself for her" (Ephesians 5:25, NIV). I remember hearing from two male individuals that their spouses had filed for divorce. I was devastated; my first question was, why? I felt such heartbreak and pain. I did not see it coming. I cried out to God, asking for divine intervention. The sad thing is they both did not have a reason for a divorce. What is even worse, they both are men and women in the church.

Malachi 2:16 (NLT) says, "For I hate divorce, says the Lord of Israel." When Jesus was asked about divorce, this was His response, "…and I say unto you, whosoever shall put away his wife, except it be for fornication, and shall marry another, committeth adultery: and whosoever marrieth her which is put away doth commit adultery" (Matthew 19:9, KJV). Search the Word of God; nothing is too big for God to handle. Let us not be phony Christians, only trying to protect our image. Don't replace God's Word with false ideology and interpretation. Place all your values in God and what He thinks of you. Caregivers, fight for your marriage. Fight for your family.

Let us pray:

Lord Jesus,

This morning, I pray for marriages and families in Jesus' name. Broken homes, mend them in the mighty name of Jesus. Father, open the hearts of men and women and grant them a heart of forgiveness, in Jesus' name. Restore unto couples the joy of their first encounter in Jesus' name. Lord, I thank You for what You are doing in homes and families right now, in Jesus' mighty name, amen.

Caregivers, let us all stand in agreement today. That wife, husband, or child is coming back home in Jesus' name. I am delegating myself a week of prayer and fasting for marriages and families in Jesus' name, amen. Shalom.

For each day of the week, write a prayer for your spouse and/or children, another's spouse and/or children to stay true to their vows and promises before God, and for those that are deceived in getting a divorce frivolously.

Day one:____________________________________

____

____

____

____

____

____

Day two:____________________________________

____

____

____

____

____

____

Day three: ______________________________

____

____

____

____

____

____

Day four: ______________________________

____

____

____

____

____

____

Day five: ______________________________

____

____

____

____

____

____

Day six: _______________________________

____

____

____

____

____

Day seven: ________________________________

____

____

____

____

____

130

Trusting God

"Trust in the Lord with all thine heart, and lean not unto thine own understanding. In all thy ways acknowledge him, and he shall direct thy path" (Proverbs 3:5–6, KJV). How many times do we try to do things on our own and don't get it right? If we don't put God in it, we cannot solve it. God desires for us to put Him first in everything. A good example; you tried to find a good job, going to interviews upon interviews, without success. Eventually, taking a job that you are not satisfied with. The salary may not be good for the amount of work. But, you take it anyway, maybe to pay the bills or to meet some other need.

Before you start your job hunt, did you go before God in prayer? Telling Him the type of job you desire, expected salary, or the kind of benefits you are expecting. These are some of the things we have to consider. Don't try to find that job on your own; tell God what you want, giving Him specifics to work with. Whatever you ask for, you will receive in Jesus' name. And this goes for many other areas of your life. Like seeking a good husband. Would you look for a husband in a club or bar? I agree the church is not the only place to find a good husband or wife. Some people may attend the house of the Lord in disguise. That's why it is important to take everything to God in prayer; He will direct your path. Whatever you may be desiring today, trust God; He will fulfill it. Just give Him a chance in Jesus' name, amen. Shalom!

131

Being bold for God

"The wicked flee when no man pursueth: but the righteous are bold as a lion" (Proverbs 28:1, KJV). We must stand for what is right regardless. People keep silent for many reasons, be it fear, shame, pride, repulsion, or retaliation. But, "For God has not given us a spirit of fear and timidity, but of power, love, and self-discipline" (2 Timothy 1:7, NLT).

Caregivers, today, I want to encourage each of you to stand boldly on the Word of God. Put God first in everything. When you go for that interview, speak up for what you are expecting in a calm, concise manner. Looking for a new home, don't just take any old place; let God choose for you. Daily, share your testimonies about the goodness of God. Encourage that sister or brother; one day, a word that you have said would resonate.

We are too dormant, allowing every and anything to take place. Remember, we don't have to get angry or argue. Correctly state the facts backed up with evidence from the Bible. God wants us to be bold for Him. We were given the authority to lay hands on the sick and make declarations in Jesus' name. There is power in the name of Jesus; use it.

I remember, one day preaching in Penn Station, New York. After I was done, a young woman came to me in tears. Her question was, "how do I get to know the Jesus you are speaking about?" With tears streaming down both our faces, I taught her to pray for redemption. I am a disciple of Jesus Christ, and I am not ashamed or timid. I know without a doubt Jesus Christ will stand up for me in my Father's house. Amen. Don't turn a blind eye; being obedient is one thing but being bold for God's kingdom is another. Stay walking by faith in Jesus' name, amen. Shalom!

____

____

____

____

____

____

132

Understanding God

Have you ever prayed to God for a blessing or miracle and never received it? Like the time when your husband or wife was terminally ill, and you did not receive a miracle to save his or her life. Or you lost your job and became homeless with your family. The outcome may not be what you hope for, but don't give up. Always remember everything happens for a reason. God sees and knows everything. He knows what tomorrow holds, so please stay in faith, and believe without a doubt that God has already done it.

Sometimes our healing has already taken place, but doubt creeps in, one of the devil's tools, causing us to give up. What good is it, caregivers, if you say you have faith but don't exercise it? Abraham is the perfect example of one who never doubts God's power. He was willing to give his own son as a sacrifice. God rewarded him for trusting in Him and his entire generation. Blessed. All because he believed and trusted God. Today, not tomorrow, let us all stand on the true *Word* of God.

Let us pray:

Heavenly Father,

I trust You for my healing in Jesus' name. That new

job that has my name on it, I claim it right now in Jesus' name. For all those who have been waiting for many years for a good Christian husband, we trust You in Jesus' name. I trust You for more wisdom and patience in Jesus' name.

I believe without a doubt that You are going to do what You say You are going to do. I pray with faith in Jesus Christ, amen. (Personalize this prayer according to your circumstances.) Continue walking by faith, in Jesus' name, amen. Shalom!

____

____

____

____

____

____

133

Blessed Friday

Stay prayerful; this is my encouragement today! Caregivers, we must always keep Jesus in our thoughts. We must wake each morning not too busy to say, "Thank You, Father." Prayer is spending quality time with God. Neither is praying one time per week or when you remember acceptable or wise. Question: Do you eat one or two times per week? Obviously, no. Just as our physical body needs nutrients, our spiritual being needs sustenance, which is the constant connection with God, amen.

Prayer is a two-way street: talking to God and listening to God. In all the chaos and confusion taking place in this world, we have to separate ourselves. God loves it when you spend quality time in His presence. I have learned over the years to live in an attitude of prayerfulness. Even when I am working, my thoughts are always on God. Allow your lifestyle to be governed by God and His *Word*. Be always expectant to hear from God in Jesus' name, amen. Shalom!

____

____

____

____

____

____

134

Expecting breakthroughs

The Bible says, "Ask and it shall be given to you; seek, and ye shall find; knock, and it shall be open to you" (Matthew 7:7, NIV).

Caregivers, now is the time for your breakthroughs. God wants us to be in constant prayer. Don't allow life's woes and worries to distract you from your relationship with your Creator. Stumbling blocks may be in your way today; I pray that it is removed in Jesus' name. God is always ready and willing to help you in your time of need. Don't hesitate; just step out in faith and receive your breakthrough in the mighty name of Jesus Christ, amen. Shalom! List your petition to *God* below, and when you get your breakthrough, come back here and tick them off:

Breakthrough #1 ________________________________

____

Breakthrough #2 ________________________________

____

Breakthrough #3 ________________________________

____

Breakthrough #4 ________________________________

____

Breakthrough #5 ________________________________

____

Breakthrough #6 ________________________________

____

Breakthrough #7 ________________________________

____

135

Good morning, caregivers!

"Speak up for those who cannot speak for themselves..." (Proverbs 31:8, NIV) This Scripture is telling us that we ought to be our brother's keepers. As I walked recently on Broadway, New York, I was aware of the huge number of homeless people sitting or lying on the dirty sidewalks. Walking by, my eyes began to search their faces; all I could see were blank expressions. Most were unaware of where they were, what time it was, and their cleanliness or lack of. My thoughts immediately were that they were someone's son, daughter, mother, father, sister, brother, aunt, or uncle. I wondered to myself what had caused them to reach this point.

We, on the other hand, are none of that. We have comfortable indoor living, choices of food to eat, clean clothes to wear, and anything else we desire. Think about how God wants us to live with one another. The next time you see someone on the ground, please think about whether it could have been you or I. How blessed we are to have Jesus Christ as our Lord and Savior. Stretch your helping hand and ask them if you can get them something to eat or drink. Seek out social help for them from NGOs and others that are willing to help those less fortunate and struggling as they are. We are our brothers' and sisters' keepers. Stay blessed in Jesus' name, amen. Shalom!

136

We serve a big God

God is so big! He rules the entire universe. His love and mercies are for everyone. God has a plan for every one of us. “For I know the thoughts that I think towards you, saith the Lord, thoughts of peace. and not of evil, to give you an expected end” (Jeremiah 29:11, KJV).

Caregivers think big. I once read a book by Ben Carson called *Dream Big*. It was very inspiring, so I passed it on to my youngest son. I really hope he reads it and it inspires him as it did for me. It is important to ask ourselves this question, “What is my purpose in this life?” It just cannot be sleeping, eating, or working, each day. We were created in our mother’s womb to be someone great.

My encouragement to each of you is to push yourself to greatness. Don’t allow complacency to get the better of you. My prayer is that the overflowing of blessings, mercies, and grace be your portion in Jesus’ name. Caregivers, step into leadership, step into high places, step into your purpose in Jesus’ name, amen. Have a wonderful day with your family in Jesus’ name, amen. Shalom!

____

____

____

____

137

Good morning, caregivers!

How we live reveals what we believe and whether the faith we profess to have is a living faith. Caregivers, don't ignore the power of having faith in Christ Jesus. There are many examples of faith at work in the Bible. It is very simple, you can start today, and if you don't quite understand how faith works, pray and start a Bible study group with church members or just your family and see God take you from a place of ignorance to one of understanding.

One example of faith could be in this situation demonstrated here: You are looking for a job, and you are trusting God to provide that job. But you have to do some work. Firstly, you prayerfully go to God with what kind of job you desire, the benefits you want, and what you are expecting. With your resumé professionally done, you begin your search. Now God loves you and knows what is your heart's desire; He will provide. You, on the other hand, would continue to stay in prayer and thanksgiving. Even if you have to wait a while, the call is coming. Although you get the job and the money is questionable, He has already secured you financially. Talk to that situation; whether it's healing or any other need, it is done in Jesus' name, amen. Shalom!

138

God Is Your Source

We awake each day either worried or concerned about something. It may be health, finances, work, or family concern. Then you spend time wastefully trying to fix things by yourself, but it only makes things worse. But rest assured, God is your source. God is your supply house. God is your healer. God is your protector. God is your everything. You can do absolutely nothing without God.

My encouragement to you today is to allow God to do His work in your life. Sometimes the enemies' tools, such as impatience and frustration, push us to make mistakes. This is what the scripture says, "[…] my God shall supply all your needs according to his riches in glory by Christ Jesus" (Philippians 4:19, KJV). Hallelujah, amen. You can personalize this prayer because God's promise is true. Trust God with your whole heart today in Jesus' name, amen. Shalom!

____

____

____

____

____

____

139

Restoring your years

God wants us to draw closer to Him. God's love for you is to be a blessing, so you will be prosperous in every way. Speak faith over every aspect of your life. The enemy wants to confuse you into thinking that you cannot have or do certain things in this life. Personalize this scripture, "I can do all things through Christ who strengthens me" (Philippians 4:13, KJV). We serve a God of life, not of sickness or death. So, don't bow to negativity; stand up with faith in Jesus Christ. Mark 11:24 (NIV) says, "Therefore I tell you, whatever you ask for in prayer, believe that you have received it, and it will be yours."

Ask God to guide you with His Holy Spirit.

> As for you, the anointing you received from him remains in you, and you do not need anyone to teach you. But as his anointing teaches you about all things and as that anointing is real, not counterfeit—just as it has taught you, remain in him.

1 John 2:27 (NIV)

Receive the gift of righteousness in Christ Jesus to everyone who believes. Have a strong and faithful day in Jesus' name, amen. Shalom!

140

The Name

Good morning, caregivers!

Do you know you have a friend whose name is Jesus Christ? He is our Lord and Savior, who is always present, amen. You don't have to be lonely anymore; just call that name. I remember one day, I had no food to feed my son at the time; he had just been released from the hospital. I looked into his beautiful eyes, so innocent, and tears began to flow from mine. I got up, filled an empty pot with water, and placed it on the stove. Next, I knelt in front of the stove and began to pray. I got emotional and wept; the only word that was released out of my mouth was the name of Jesus!

Between sobs, I just continued to repeat that name, Jesus. Then I heard the doorbell ring. Upon opening the door, I saw two friends standing there with two large bags of groceries. I invited them in to tell them my story, and they were amazed. When they were leaving, they both gave me twenty-five dollars. God heard my cry; I know there is power in the name of Jesus. Be encouraged today, caregivers. There is healing in the name of Jesus, forgiveness in the name of Jesus, and healing in the name of Jesus. Today, whatever you are facing, just call on the name of Jesus. Have a Blessed day in Jesus' name, amen. Shalom!

Call the name of your Savior, His name is: _________

_______________________________________.

141

Good morning, caregivers!

Be encouraged. Stay strong, knowing that you serve a God who will do any and everything for you. As you begin your daily duties, allow God to take the lead.

Let us read the Word of God together:

> He will cover you with his feathers.
> He will shelter you with his wings.
> His faithful promises are your armor and protection.
> Do not be afraid of the terrors of the night,
> nor the arrow that flies in the day.
> Do not dread the disease that stalks in darkness,
> nor the disaster that strikes at midday.
> Though a thousand fall at your side,
> though ten thousand are dying around you,
> these evils will not touch you.

Psalm 91:4–7 (NLT)

Go with the grace of God in Jesus' name, amen. Shalom! What is this scripture saying to you?

____

____

____

____

____

____

142

Loving God

Good morning, caregivers!

Another day, and we are still standing, thank God.

Let's read this Psalm of thanksgiving together:

> Give thanks to the LORD, for he is good. His love endures forever. Give thanks to the God of gods. His love endures forever. Give thanks to the Lord of lords: His love endures forever. To him who alone does great wonders, His love endures forever. Who by his understanding made the heavens, His love endures forever. Who spread out the earth upon the waters, His love endures forever. Who made the great lights—His love endures forever. The sun to govern the day, His love endures forever. The moon and stars to govern the night; His love endures forever. To him who struck down the firstborn of Egypt, His love endures forever. and brought Israel out from among them. His love endures forever. With a mighty hand and outstretched arm, His love endures forever. To him who divided the Red Sea asunder, His love endures forever. And brought Israel through the midst of it. His love endures forever. But swept Pharaoh and his army into the Red Sea; His love endures forever. To him who led his people through the wilderness, His love

> endures forever. To him who struck down great kings, His love endures forever. And killed mighty kings— His love endures forever. Sihon, king of the Amorites, His love endures forever. And Og king of Bashan— His love endures forever. And gave their land as an inheritance. His love endures forever. An inheritance to his servant Israel. His love endures forever. He remembered us in our low estate. His love endures forever. And freed us from our enemies. His love endures forever. He gives food to every creature. His love endures forever. Give thanks to the God of heaven. His love endures forever.

Psalm 136:1–26 (NIV)

God's love for us is everlasting, so trust God today for everything. Have a wonderful day in Jesus' name, amen. Shalom! Think about your God described here in this scripture. How does this make you feel?

____

____

____

____

____

____

143

Good morning, caregivers!

> Go into all the world and preach the gospel to all creation. Whoever believes and is baptized will be saved, but whoever does not believe will be condemned. And these signs will accompany those who believe: In my name they will drive out demons; they will speak in new tongues; they will pick up snakes with their hands; and when they drink deadly poison, it will not hurt them at all; they will place their hands on sick people, and they will get well.

Mark 16:15–18 (NIV)

As believers, we were granted the power to make commands in the name of Jesus and watch miracles happen, amen. Don't allow the devil to whisper negative thoughts like you cannot do this or that you're not good enough. Always remember you are a chosen generation and need to stand on the *Word* of God. My point today is to establish yourself in God's righteousness, no matter what the voice of accusation says. Talk to yourself, "I can do all things through Christ who strengthens me" (Philippians 4:13, NKJV). Stay focused on Jesus Christ. God loves you, I love you, and Jesus is Lord. Amen. Shalom!

144

Abrahamic blessings

Now the LORD had said to Abram:
Get out of your country,
From your family
And from your father's house,
To a land that I will show you. I will make you a great nation;
I will bless you
And make your name great;
And you shall be a blessing. I will bless those who bless you,
And I will curse him who curses you;
And in you all the families of the earth shall be blessed.

Genesis 12:1–3 (NKJV)

My encouragement to you is, don't sabotage what God has already done. The price for our sins against God was already paid years ago when Jesus died on the cross. Trust God and receive your blessings in Jesus' almighty name. I pray that you and your family will have a truly wonderful day in Jesus Christ, amen. Shalom!

____

____

____

____

____

____

145

Another day, caregivers!

Let us read this scripture together:

> Hear my cry, O God, listen to my prayer; from the end of the earth I call to you when my heart is faint. Lead me to the rock that is higher than I, for you have been my refuge, a strong tower against the enemy.
>
> Psalm 61:1–3 (ESV)

How many times do you feel alone and don't know what to say or do? You are not alone; it happens to all of us at one time or another. This is the time when you call upon the Lord your God.

Let us pray:

Heavenly Father,

I come to You just as I am. Today I am overwhelmed with life trials. So I cry out to You, knowing that You love me. I acknowledge You; You gave Your life on the cross for me. There is no other place to turn but to You, Lord. Be my peace that passes all understanding. Thank You, Jesus, for being my firm foundation. In Jesus' name, amen.

God hears and answers prayer; you can call on Him anytime and anywhere. Have a wonderful day in Jesus' name, amen. Shalom!

146

Good morning, caregivers!

Have you ever gone through difficult situations or terrible circumstances and realized how much you have matured from your past self? There's something about suffering that draws us closer to God. If life goes well all the time, we start to rely more on ourselves rather than on God. Then all we say is: I did this, and I did that; instead of Jesus did this for me. Not that God desires us to suffer always, but in our suffering, we begin to depend on Him, and He is able to show wondrous things impossible to man.

Caregivers, Jesus came so that He could exchange Himself for our shame, our suffering, and our pain. He came into this world to bear our pain and shame. After His sacrifice on that cross, our sins hold us hostage no more; we are not destined to certain death, but we have an escape in Christ, amen. John 10:10 (KJV) correctly states the reason, "[…] I come that they might have life, and that they might have it more abundantly."

This is the good news of Christ. After the death penalty, Jesus arose from the grave, hallelujah! Leaving mankind free to serve God our Heavenly Father, amen. If you have never totally believed it before, try placing all your trust in God today. Whatever valley you are in at the moment, you will come out in the name of Jesus. Test gives us testimony, amen. Your victory is here in Jesus' name, amen. Shalom! What do you believe Him for today:

____

____

____

____

____

____

147

Good morning, caregivers!

What are you worshiping?

Is it your husband, wife, children, new wardrobe, new car, fat bank account, a boyfriend, jewelry, even sex, whatever it is, remember, we serve a jealous God. Don't misunderstand; it's nice to have the luxuries of life. But they are not your God. There is a difference between love and worship. We all have a loved one that we strive to provide for, love, and cherish. But, there is a time when we must separate ourselves from them and the things of this world to put God first. God comes before spouse, children, parents, wealth, power, and position. God is who He is; He created us in His image and likeness for His will. Aligning ourselves to the will of God should be our purpose in life; try Him and see that it is worth it. Our mission as believers is to worship God in spirit and truth and enjoy the beauty of this Earth, in Jesus' name, amen. Shalom! List the things you have been putting before God today and strike them out on this page and in your hearts as you strive to serve God fully in Spirit and in truth:

___

___

___

148

Good morning, caregivers!

Let us go before the throne of God with our praise.

Let us pray:

Dear Lord,

Thank You for allowing us to see this new day. You woke us up this morning, and for that, we are thankful. Continue to strengthen us daily as we leave our respective homes. Guide us in everything we do. May we make accurate decisions guided by Your hands, Lord. Bless those in authority over us, that we may have respect for each other in Jesus' name. Take us to and from our individual jobs safely, in Jesus' name, amen.

Caregivers, my encouragement to you today is to stand on the *Word* of God.

Learn to forgive others, love more, trust in God more, be obedient, stay humble, and bless in Jesus' love. Have a fabulous day, in Jesus' name, amen. Shalom!

149

Good morning, caregivers!

These are troubling times we are living in, and mankind is going too far.

Let us remember what happened in the days of Sodom and Gomorrah and the days of Noah. God looked upon men and women that He had created and was greatly disappointed. In His disappointment, except for Noah and his family, He destroyed the entire Earth and its content. Let us not forget that God sent His only Son, Jesus, to die for our sins. He arose from the grave and ascended into heaven with a promise to come again, but mankind is never satisfied.

God is about to return to the Earth again. The question is, Are you ready? Are you prepared to meet your Heavenly Father? Caregivers, God is giving us plenty of time to prepare our hearts to meet Him. Some may think it is a joke as the years roll by. But God's Word is true. It is written:

> Let not your hearts be troubled. Believe in God; believe also in me. In my Father's house there are many rooms. If it were not so, would I have told you that? I go to prepare a place for you? And if I go and prepare a place for you, I will come again and will take you to myself, that where I am you may be also.

John 14:1–3 (ESV)

Caregivers, get ready, serve God in Spirit, and in truth, for our days are numbered. Have a wonderful day with your loved ones in Jesus' name, amen. Shalom!

____

____

____

____

____

____

150

Having confidence in God

> I cried out, I am slipping!
> but your unfailing love, O Lord, supported me.
> When doubts filled my mind,
> Your comfort gave me renewed hope and cheer.

Psalm 94:18–19 (NLT)

Sometimes you can feel like life is a struggle; everything keeps going wrong. It's like from one thing to the other, a breakdown car, family confusion, children disobeying…, and you want to just throw your hands up in the air and scream.

If that's you this morning, you are not alone.

Let us pray:

Dear God,

I pray for Your presence; I feel like I cannot bear it anymore. Let me feel Your sweet embrace; at times, I feel weak. Give me the strength to face whatever comes my way with confidence in You. I know You are with me always; help me to remember You are my strength. Thank You for hearing and answering my prayer in Jesus' name, amen.

In this life that we are living in, challenges will surely confront us; no one is exempt. What should we do? Should we turn to man for answers? No, man and science cannot solve things. Our only choice is to turn to God, amen. Seek His face and pray for His help. Without a doubt, God answers all our prayers. Caregivers, God loves you; God loves all of us. Stay confident in His love. You can personalize this prayer above and add it as needed in Jesus' name, amen. Shalom!

____

____

____

____

____

____

151

Communicating with God is simple

Many times I will get this complaint from others; I don't know how to pray. And I would say it's not difficult at all. I do understand that as a new convert, sometimes nervousness sets in. But by all means, don't let the nerve get the better of you. A church sister or brother may use certain scripture quotes in their prayer that may make you think, "Oh Lord, I cannot express myself like him or her." Always remember, prayer is talking to God. Thanking Him for everything, placing all your worries and concerns on Him. Don't worry; God is a big God but is concerned about our little matters as well. As a matter of fact, He is not just your God; He is the God of the entire world.

Let us pray:

Lord, I praise You for Your great love for me and Your power that works on my behalf. Help me to trust You more and more today. I lay down all of my worries at Your feet. I surrender my life to Your control. Use me, Lord, for Your honor and glory. Take full control of my life. I am human, but You are God, the Great "I Am." Guide and direct my steps in Jesus' name, amen. Shalom!

152

Good morning, caregivers!

Another day in Jesus' name.

Ever woke up with a song in your heart, and throughout the day, you kept singing or humming it over and over? It happens to me from time to time. Lately, I catch myself composing as I go along. Psalm 28:7 (NLT) comes to mind, "The LORD is my strength and shield. I trust him with all my heart. He helps me, and my heart is filled with joy. I burst out in songs of thanksgiving."

I know the day may be tough for many of us who are commuting to and from work but find joy in your work. Instead of getting angry, choose to be happy. Look at that person who is stressing you out straight in the eyes and tell them how much you love and appreciate them. Let us be like the psalmist David and choose to be happy. When worries come, sing; when problems confront you, sing; when you feel sad, just sing. It really works. I pray that these few words uplift you throughout your day and always. May God's peace be with you always in Jesus' name. Shalom!

___

___

___

___

___

153

Good morning, caregivers!

The Lord is our shepherd.

When one thinks of a shepherd, the first thing that comes to mind is sheep. A shepherd looks after his flocks; if any of them stray, he will go looking until he finds it. It is the same thing with God, He is our Shepherd, and we are His sheep. God will do anything for us. He is always there to look after us, tending to our needs.

Sometimes we acknowledge God, and sometimes we don't. I want to encourage you today to stay close to your heavenly Shepherd. Don't allow the distractions of this world to cause you to stray. The world has nothing to offer but shame, sickness, and disgrace.

Let us pray:

Dear Jesus,

Thank You for being my shepherd. When I stray from You, Lord, You always come looking. I pray that I stay close to You, never wandering away. Father, keep Your staff of protection over me and my household in Jesus' name, amen.

Caregivers, be encouraged and allow God to shepherd you today. Stay close to your flock in Jesus' name, amen. Shalom!

____

____

____

____

____

____

154

Good morning, caregivers, find your peace!

Many times we worry about the bills, children, health, and family. Do you know that God doesn't want us to live in a state of worry? Physical and mental stress is not good for mankind. But the devil and his fallen angels are loose upon this Earth. He is influencing and conquering mankind because we spend too much time worrying instead of fortifying ourselves with God's Word. In times such as these, we need God. Get in that quiet corner at home or the bathroom and cry out to God. God answers all of our cares, amen.

Caregivers, when you wake up in the morning, firstly pray, then spend time reading the Word of God. Then you will experience the best life of all. People will enquire about you, wondering why you are always happy. Find your peace and joy in Abba Father today. Allow that peace that passeth all understanding to take control over your lives in Jesus' name. Have a wonderful day in Jesus' mighty name, amen. Shalom!

____

____

____

____

____

____

155

Good morning, caregivers!

Praise God!

I awoke this morning with such joy, knowing that I am still alive and loved by God; to God be the glory. There are many who went to bed last night, and their eyes did not open this morning.

Thank You, Lord, for Your mercies towards us.

Let us pray:

Heavenly Father,

I just want to say thanks! There are not enough words on my lips to express my gratitude towards You. Jesus, keep us all in good health in this land of the living. I am ever thankful to see the rising of the sun on another day; forever and ever, amen.

Today let us share the joy of life with each other in Jesus' name, amen. Shalom!

____

____

____

____

____

____

156

Good morning, caregivers!

God is Love.

How do I know God is Love? Because the Bible tells me He is Love. Let us read the Word of the Lord together:

> Beloved, let us love one another, for love is of God, and everyone who loves is born of God and knows God. He who does not love does not know God, because God is love. In this the love of God was manifested toward us, that God has sent His only begotten Son into the world, that we might live through him. In this is love, not that we loved God, but that He loved us and sent his Son to be the propitiation for our sins. Beloved, If God so loved us, we also ought to love one another. No one has ever seen God at any time. If we love one another, God abides in us, and His love has been perfected in us.

1 John 4:7–12 (NKJV)

Love could be described as a deep affection for someone or something; examples are the love for spouse, parents, children, family, and friends. But, let us not forget the men, women, and children who are without shelter, food, clothing, or love. Most of them are sleeping on the streets. Something traumatic may have happened to make them be in that position.

Caregivers, we are to reach out to that sister or brother and let them know that you love them. Ask them how you can be of assistance to them. Remember, God loves you, and Jesus is Lord over all, so share His love to others so they can know Him and be built up by Him. He won't force Himself on anyone, but with a willing and open heart ready to receive Him, He can work things out for their good, amen. Shalom!

____

____

____

____

____

____

157

Good morning, caregivers!

Here are some specific instructions. Let us read God's Word together:

> Therefore put on the full armor of God, so that when the day of evil comes, you may be able to stand your ground, and after you have done everything, to stand. Stand firm then, with the belt of truth buckled around your waist, with the breastplate of righteousness in place, and with your feet fitted with the readiness that comes from the gospel of peace. In addition to all this, take up the shield of faith, with which you can extinguish all the flaming arrows of the evil one. Take the helmet of salvation and the sword of the Spirit, which is the word of God.

Ephesians 6:13–17 (NIV)

Caregivers, God is preparing us as a body of Christ for the tribulation to come. But have no fear if you have been preparing. We are living in troubling times. The horrendous display is unfolding right before our very eyes. As Christians, we should not fear because we obey.

Let us pray.

Jesus, You have not given us a fearful mine, so all of

our trust is placed in You. We will walk in obedience according to Your Word. With faith in Jesus Christ, amen. Shalom!

____

____

____

____

____

____

158

Good morning, caregivers!

A new day in your life.

"For I know the plans I have for you, declares the Lord, plans for welfare and not for evil, to give you a future and a hope" (Jeremiah 29:11, NLT). Many times we hold on past hurts, repeatedly reliving them. God wants you to trust Him at His Word and let it go. "Remember not the former things, nor consider the things of old. Behold, I am doing a new thing; now it springs forth, do you not perceive it? I will make a way in the wilderness and rivers in the desert" (Isaiah 43:18–19, NLT).

My friend, don't waste another moment replaying the tape recordings in your head. Instead, replace it with good thoughts and good memories. I love sharing my testimony with others because it is my testimony of God's blessings. This is God's plan for us; let's read together:

> And if you faithfully obey the voice of the LORD your God, being careful to do all his commandments that I command you today, the LORD your God will set you high above all the nations of the earth. And all these blessings shall come upon you and overtake you if you obey the voice of the Lord your God.
>
> Blessed shall you be in the city, and blessed

> shall you be in the field.
> Blessed shall be the fruit of your womb and the fruit of your ground and the fruit of your cattle, the increase of your herds and the young of your flock.
> Blessed shall be your basket and your kneading bowl. Blessed shall you be when you come in, and blessed shall you be when you go out.

Deuteronomy 28:1–6 (ESV)

Let us pray.

Heavenly Father,

I pray for each and every one who may be confused by negative thoughts. I pray for total deliverance in Jesus' name. Guide and direct their steps to a position of positive thinking. May their heart be at peace at all times, knowing God has a plan of blessings for them. May the saving grace of God be with us always, amen.

Have a wonderful day today in Jesus Christ, amen. Shalom!

____

____

____

____

____

____

159

Caregivers

Prayer changes things.

The Bible says, "Do not be anxious about anything, but in every situation, by prayer and petition, with thanksgiving, present your requests to God. And the peace of God, which transcends all understanding, will guard your hearts and your minds in Christ Jesus." (Philippians 4:6–7, NIV). Today, if you are in need of breakthroughs, take it to God in prayer. "And pray in the Spirit on all occasions, with all kinds of prayers and requests. With this in mind, be alert and always keep on praying for all the Lord's people" (Ephesians 6:18, NIV).

In your prayers, give thanks to God for what He has done, exercising your faith, considering it done in Jesus' name. "Give thanks in all circumstances; for this is God's will for you in Christ Jesus" (1 Thessalonians 5:18, NIV).

Let us pray.

Dear Jesus,

We thank You this day for what You are working out for our good in Jesus' name.

You said, Lord, that if we have faith as small as a mus-

tard seed, we can move mountains. We are standing on Your Word and consider it done in Jesus' mighty name, amen. Shalom!

____

____

____

____

____

____

160

Caregivers

You are not alone.

"Have I not commanded you? Be strong and courageous. Do not be frightened, and do not be dismayed, for the Lord your God is with you wherever you go" (Joshua 1:9, NIV). God speaks with authority, wanting us to place all our trust in Him. At times you may feel disappointed and alone, but you are not. Dig in your heels and meditate on God's Word until you receive your breakthrough.

You are victorious and destined to win by God's grace. The devil's tools are lies, upon lies to deceive you, but pay him no attention. Instead, focus on the true promises of our almighty God, who is our strength. Have a wonderful day and a Blessed day in our Lord and Savior Jesus Christ, amen. Shalom!

____

____

____

____

____

____

161

Caregivers

A new day in Christ.

"This is the day the LORD has made. We will rejoice and be glad in it" (Psalm 118:24, NLT). Ever got home at the end of the day after work feeling exhausted, sore, irritated, and short-tempered? You can barely get anything done; all you are thinking of is the bed. Does it sound like a joyful day to you?

Caregivers, we need to take better care of ourselves mentally, physically, and spiritually. Do creative things that would help you relax and be at peace with yourself. Take God at His Word; He desires the best for you. God will give you that inner joy that would shine on the outside. God has the best plan for our lives, where happiness and joy rule. So caregivers, let us choose joy and gladness over sadness. Begin your day in the presence of God, and you will have a peaceful day in Jesus' name, amen. Shalom! Plan something fun to do with your family and friends this weekend and put effort to get it done:

____

____

____

____

____

162

Being thankful

First Thessalonian 5:18 (KJV) states, "In every thing give thanks: for this is the will of God in Christ Jesus concerning you." God's plan is to bless us, no matter what, but many times we are the ones who prevent our blessings from taking place. We get very complacent, forgetting to thank God.

Let us pray.

Lord Jesus,

I thank You for each and every one who is reading this message. May Your supply house always be available to us in Jesus' name. Bless them and their household in the overflow in Jesus' name.

Abba Father, continue to uplift us spiritually and physically in Jesus' mighty name, amen. Shalom!

____

____

____

____

____

____

163

Caregivers

A prayer of thanksgiving.

Let us pray:

God, You are good, and Your everlasting love surrounds us. You have given Your angels charge over us daily so we may work to provide. Keep us honest and true to Your Word lest we fall into temptation. As we receive our wages, Lord, help us to remember to honor You with our first fruit, which is our tithes and offering in Jesus' name. Bless our employers in every possible way so that they will appreciate us with extra blessings. Use us as caregivers to touch and change the hearts of employers in Jesus' name. Right now, Father, pour down showers of blessings upon each and everyone reading this prayer, in Jesus' name, amen. Have a wonderful day with your family and friends in Jesus' name. Almighty amen. Shalom!

____

____

____

____

____

____

164

God our Comforter

Paul teaches the church in Corinth, "Blessed be God, even the Father of our Lord Jesus Christ, the Father of mercies and God of all comfort; Who comforteth us in all our tribulations, that we may be able to comfort them which are in trouble, by wherewith we ourselves are comforted of God" (2 Corinthians 1:3–4, KJV). Caregivers, God's blessings are contagious, and His purpose is for us to share our blessings with others.

Put on your thinking cap and think about who in your surroundings is in direct need of your blessings. Is it the waiter who is serving you or the person cleaning your streets? Think! And then act as the Holy Spirit leads. Amen. Starting today, reach out to someone, and please bless them from your heart. I will also like to encourage everyone to read and study the Bible, which is God's living Word.

Let us pray.

Dear Jesus,

Thank You for Your Word! Thank You for life itself. Thank You for each other. Thank You for all added blessings seen and unseen in Jesus' mighty name, amen. Shalom!

165

Good morning, caregivers!

Let us give thanks.

Heavenly Father,

Firstly, thank You, Lord, for the opportunity to enjoy Your beauty. With each new day, our hope in You is renewed. With Your continuing protection over my family, my co-workers, my friends, and my employers, I gain the strength to fight. I learn to trust and depend on You and You alone. When thoughts of failure come, I replace them with faith-filled words. Help me to be a good servant to Your Word. I have found a place of peace knowing that I have a Heavenly Father who loves me. I pray that You use me, Lord, to Your honor and glory in Jesus' name. My main goal in this life is to abide by Your Word. I am grateful You have accepted me back into Your fold. I can boldly say I was blind; now I see I was weak, but now I'm strong in You. Continue to bless me and all who are repeating this prayer with me with more wisdom. Keep us humble and meek in Jesus' name, amen.

Caregivers, receive your blessing today in Jesus' name, amen. Shalom!

____

____

166

Caregivers

Perseverance in the face of condemnation.

"The Lord saw that the wickedness of man was great on the Earth and that every intent of the thoughts of his heart was only evil continually" (Genesis 6:5, ESV). We may live in this world, but we don't have to be of the world. There is too much chaos and confusion taking place, and if we are not careful, we could easily get caught up in it. The Bible tells us about guarding our hearts against negative persuasion. Let us, as believers, stand out and be different and pray to God for change.

Lately, there has been a rapid increase of theories and ideologies trying to persuade us against God's Word. The Bible and Christianity are being criticized and misinterpreted openly because the same critics have an agenda. Let us stay in continued prayer to be overcomers. Noah was jeered and made fun of for many years before the flood came. But when the day finally came, only Noah and his family, who believed in the Words of God, were saved.

Remember to pray for the decision-makers in society and the many heads of government in the world. Hasty and hash decisions have been made to satisfy their own agendas. But God is watching and waiting to put in His appearance to judge.

Let us pray.

Lord,

Thank You for the confirmation of Your Word. We have Your protection to keep us safe in times like these. Keep us, Your children, rooted and grounded in You, the True Living God.

Today, we are encouraged to trust the power of God's love. Have a truly beautiful day in Jesus' name, amen. Shalom!

____

____

____

____

____

____

167

Renewal of Self

Ephesians 4:22–23 (NLT) says, "Throw off your old sinful nature and your former way of life, which is corrupted by lust and deception. Instead, let the Spirit renew your thoughts and attitudes." Caregivers, before we are "born again," there are things we accept and habits we adopt. Many times, condoning wrongdoing, lies, thievery, fornication, adultery, and the like. But after we were "born again" Christians, the Holy Spirit began to work on the inside.

Let us look at the life of Paul as an example. His former name was Saul; he was a persecutor of Christians. Until the day that God stopped him. His entire life was changed, including his name. At the end, Paul was imprisoned for preaching and teaching the Gospel of Christ Jesus and was later put to death for it. However, even unto his death, Paul encouraged the church body of Christ to stand strong for the Lord.

All Christians have a serious role to play on this Earth. We have to stand in unity and spread the good news of the Gospel. Let us press forward, never looking back to the "old self" because today, you are a new person in Christ. Study your Bible for more insight. I pray for the renewal of the Holy Spirit within us in Jesus' name, amen. Shalom!

Who were you:

____

____

____

____

____

____

Who are you now:

____

____

____

____

____

____

168

Pleasant morning, caregivers!

Christian faith:

> Whatever happens, conduct yourselves in a manner worthy of the gospel of Christ. Then, whether I come and see you or only hear about you in my absence, I will know that you stand firm in the one Spirit, striving together as one for the faith of the gospel.

Philippians 1:27 (NIV)

Being a Christian doesn't mean that we'll be exempt from facing tragedies or hardships. But what it does mean is that in the midst of our difficulties, we can experience Christian happiness. Paul, a servant of God, wrote many letters from behind the prison wall. It comes down to something the apostle Paul frequently referred to when he was writing to the believers in Philippi. The Christian faith is a happy faith and a hopeful faith.

We have hope in this life and in our relationship with the Lord, and we have hope for the afterlife. But this doesn't mean that Christians are happy all the time or that we should walk around wearing fake smiles. The secret of Christian happiness is found in the way that we think, not in the way that we feel. So if we want to be happy, then just be. Every action starts with a thought. And what we think is what we'll do.

Today, let us keep the Word of God written in our hearts. True happiness can only come from God's blessings. Believers always remember what Romans 10:17 (KJV) says, "So faith comes from hearing, and hearing through the word of Christ." Have a wonderful day, trusting our Lord and Savior Jesus Christ, amen. Shalom!

____

____

____

____

____

____

169

Allow God to fight your battle

> Everyone assembled here will know that the Lord rescues his people, but not with sword and spear. This is the Lord's battle, and he will give you to us! As Goliath moved closer to attack, David quickly ran out to meet him.

1 Samuel 17:47–48 (NLT)

Many times in our lives, we allow fear to dominate us. Always thinking I cannot do that or there is no way I can accomplish this. We serve the only True and Living God that reminds us daily, "I can do all things through Christ who strengthens me" (Philippians 3:13).

Let us pray!

Heavenly Father,

Help us to remember that Your perfect love casts out fear. I pray that our obedience to You and Your will is never compromised by our fear and attempts to flee from what we know is right to do. Right now, I command the Goliaths in our lives to be removed in Jesus' name. Amen.

Trust God for and with everything. He is our Father, our friend, our everything. Have a bold day in Jesus' name, amen. Shalom!

170

Living by Faith and Not by Sight

Second Corinthians 5:7 (NIV) says, "For we live by faith, not by sight." Living in the end times requires living by faith and not by what we see going on around us. Don't be sidetracked or distracted. Keeping our eyes set on what is happening in the physical world will prevent us from seeing and believing what God is doing in the spiritual. This morning, let us give thanks unto God for His protection and all that He has already done.

Let us pray.

Heavenly Father,

Thank You for another day, for the opportunity to open our eyes to enjoy the beauty of You. Bless each and every one reading this simple prayer in Jesus' name. Abundantly, supply all their needs according to Your riches in glory. Protect their homes, jobs, marriage, children, family, finances, and good health in Jesus' name. Lord, we look to You for everything. I pray everyone will be abundantly blessed in the overflow for their hard work in Jesus' mighty name, amen. Shalom!

171

From bondage to freedom

Are you searching for God today? In the midst of all the confusion, chaos, pain, suffering, sickness, and even death, remember God is in the midst. Just open up your heart and let Him in

Repeat this simple prayer.

Jesus, today, I believe You died for my sins. I accept You as my Lord and Savior. Come into my heart, Lord. Make me a new person in Christ. Thank You for forgiving me. Thank You for accepting me. From this day forward, I will live for You in Jesus' name, amen.

If you just prayed that prayer for the first time, ask God to lead you to His church and make it your home. Stay focused and bless, amen. Shalom!

____

____

____

____

____

____

172

Good morning, caregivers!

It is a thankful day, praise God. Do you feel excited? I am. There should be a new level of expectation each morning when we awake. Expectations of renewed confidence, hope for betterment, increased blessings, and favor. You see, the devil wants total control on this Earth. He is a joy stealer, family destroyer, confusion maker, murderer, and more if we allow him. So he tries his best to trick you into thinking evil.

It is important to read and study the Word of God so that we all can recalibrate ourselves in times of misgiving. Those trying times will not last forever. Equipped with God's Word, repeating them constantly and daily, I can do all things through Christ. I am the head and never the tail, above always and never beneath. God is my supply house and will supply all my needs.

Abba Father, You are my provider; I trust You for everything. These are only some of the phrases you can constantly say when you are communicating with your maker. Without a doubt, we are living in perilous times. The second coming of Jesus Christ is sooner than we expect. The discouragers will tell you, "So long we heard that God is coming, where is He?" The liberals, seculars, atheists, and other modernist idealists will try to change your minds with their own philosophy, theology, theory, and ideas. Believers in Jesus Christ, stand your ground.

Stay in prayer, be safe in Jesus' name, amen. Shalom!

____

____

____

____

____

____

Gabriel

Everyone calls her "Gabby" or Gabriel. Her mom brought her to the United States when she was just ten years old on a tourist visa. Like everyone else, they stayed to pursue their dreams. After many years of working as a babysitter, her mom developed breast cancer. She was treated and told that it went into remission. Two years later, cancer returned, which took her. Gabby, at the time, had just turned eighteen and was part of the DACA program put in place by President Obama at the time.

Gabby's mother died, leaving her as an only child in a house in Queens, New York, with a very high mortgage. In her time of need, all of Gabby's aunt and uncle, who were living in the house, moved out. The house was foreclosed by the bank, and Gabby was left with no place to live. Thanks to the pastor of the church her late mother used to attend, they took her in. She developed health problems of her own.

One day she called me crying, concerned I prayed with her and then listened to her. She was diagnosed with multiple sclerosis and sickle cell anemia. To make matters worse, she was homeless for a while until a stranger felt sorry and took her in. There is an old saying, "When it rains, it pours." In this situation, it seems like everything went wrong with Gabby.

At twenty-one years old, unable to perform everyday habits without help from a Home Health Aid (HHA), Gabby still thinks it could have been worse. She survived COVID-19 and is currently living with her late mother's only brother. My daily words of encouragement are what keep Gabby strong each day, praise God. She is praying that God will make way for her in the storms of life.

173

Year of greatness

> So put to death the sinful, earthly things lurking within you. Have nothing to do with sexual immorality, impurity, lust, and evil desires. Don't be greedy, for a greedy person is an idolater, worshiping the things of this world. Because of these sins, the anger of God is coming. You used to do these things when your life was still part of this world. But now is the time to get rid of anger, rage, malicious behavior, slander, and dirty language. Don't lie to each other, for you have stripped off your old sinful nature and all its wicked deeds.

Colossians 3:5–9 (NLT)

Before encountering Jesus, we lived for ourselves and may have behaved or had thoughts that were not of God. If we're honest, there are times, as Christians, we still struggle in these areas described above. However, it's clear that we need to make daily choices to put to death what does not glorify God. It's not something to do in our own ability—we are simply not able to do it on our own, and that is one of the many reasons why we need Jesus!

Let us pray.

Dear God,

Many times we don't deserve Your forgiveness. Day after day, we sin, and we fall short of what You have for us. We are unworthy of Your mercy, but You offer it to us each morning.

Thank You, Lord, that when we repent and ask for forgiveness, You remember our sins no more (Hebrews 8:12). Lord, although we still remember and still hold on to hurt, You have given us the greatest example of forgiveness. You sent Your Son to walk the same Earth we walk, to experience the same hurt and betrayal we do, and yet He chose to forgive.

Help us to follow Jesus' example. Remind us that prayer is one of our greatest weapons, and through continual prayer, praying for our enemies, You will begin to soften our hearts and give us the strength to forgive them.

Help us see those who have hurt us the same way You see them. Help us to have compassion for them.

Father, bless those who have wronged us. Show us where we are still holding back forgiveness so that we can begin the obedient steps of forgiving. As this new year quickly approaches, grant us a new desire to serve You. Father, many times, we get disappointed and discouraged.

Give us a heart committed to serving You in spirit and in truth. Thank You, Lord, for Your unconditional love.

Have a wonderful day of unlimited blessings in Jesus Christ, amen. Shalom!

Make a list below of your expectations for this new day:

____

____

____

____

____

____

174

Praying with purpose

Many of us, at times, fall into one of these categories:

- Not enough time, so we rush to work or meeting, distracted by others.
- Or too tired of having errands to run, appointments, and other engagements.

My encouragement to you this day is to renew your commitment to spend quality time with God. Place your faith in Jesus Christ; it changes everything.

Let us pray.

Dear Lord,

I bring my prayer life before You; many times, I allow worldly things to distract me from You. Help me to stay focused and always put you first. My prayer today is for a renewed commitment to serving You in Spirit and truth. Reveal unto me, Lord, ways I can be of service to Your kingdom and Your glory. Help me to walk the straight and narrow pathway to heaven. Keep a great fire burning within my heart to spread the Gospel, the true living Word of Jesus Christ. Use me, Lord, allow me to be a blessing, not a hindrance to all I come in contact with daily, in Jesus' name, amen. Shalom!

____

____

____

____

____

____

175

Renewal of your faith

"Now faith is confidence in what we hope for and assurance about what we do not see" (Hebrews 11:1, NIV). As I look back to last year, in my little sphere of the world, it was tough. Death, rejection, sickness, relational discord, and violence ravaging the lives of many people I know, including myself. The experience was painful to watch and endure. But love, joy, hope, faith, and the promise of a new day comforted me.

I've been praying a lot for that new day, for God to make beauty out of the ashes, and in those prayers, I feel nothing but hope for the years ahead. Regardless of what happens today, I'm expecting God to do some pretty amazing things. And I'm hopeful that with this fresh start, my faith will only continue to strengthen and grow. I'm hoping this for you too.

Don't be deceived by discouraging words. As a matter of fact, stand only on the Word of God and live by God's Word. Doubt will only retard your true blessings. Today is the day to have confidence in God's Word. Don't waste another minute trying to accomplish things by yourself. If God is not in it, you should not have it. You may have made new resolutions about diet, sleep, exercise, etc.; take it to God in prayer first. Put your faith to work in the God of the universe. Make every new day and a new year filled with faith and finish the work of Jesus Christ. Amen. Shalom!

____

____

____

____

____

____

176

Caregivers

God has a plan for you (Part 1).

> The Lord bless you and keep you;
> the Lord make his face shine on you and be gracious to you;
> the Lord turn his face toward you
> and give you peace.

Numbers 6:24–26 (NIV)

It is not by accident you are reading these words today. Many times we doubt our potential that we were born with. Stumbling through life, making mistakes after mistakes. It is called "searching while pretending." Human beings are good at pretending while our insides are torn apart. The outside world may see a smile, but it is like a Band-Aid on a sore. The sore is sweating and creating pus, just waiting to be exposed. The moment you remove the band-aid, the sore begins to dry up and heal.

I want to let you know today that you can be who God wants you to be. No more fear, no more hiding. You were beautifully made by God our Father. You have the greater one who lives inside of you—yes, you. Receive your blessings today in Jesus' Christ, amen. Shalom!

177

God have a plan for you (Part 2).

"Before I formed you in the womb I knew you, before you were born I set you apart; I appointed you as a prophet to the nations" (Jerimiah 1:5, NIV). It is no accident you were placed on this Earth. You were beautifully and wonderfully made to dominate and rule in high places, amen. You should be very excited; I am. What do you do with that knowledge? Do you allow doubt, indecision, hopelessness, insecurities, low self-esteem, and the like to control you? I don't think so.

In the midst of your trials, laugh out loud, knowing that God's got you. Today, not tomorrow, think about the things you would like to accomplish. Make a list, pray over it and watch God fulfill it all in Jesus' name. Never allow poverty and hardship to keep you down. You can be the next Ben Carson, one of America's top neurosurgeons. My encouragement to you today is don't settle for less. Tell yourself, "I can do all things through Christ which strengthens me" (Philippians 4:13, KJV). You were uniquely created to fulfill God's purpose for your life. Success is awaiting, in Jesus' name, amen. Shalom!

____

____

178

Keep your eyes on Jesus

Hebrews 12:2–4 (ESV) says:

> Looking to Jesus, the founder and perfecter of our faith, who for the joy that was set before him endured the cross, despising the shame, and is seated at the right hand of the throne of God.
> Consider him who endured from sinners such hostility against himself, so that you may not grow weary or fainthearted. In your struggle against sin you have not yet resisted to the point of shedding your blood.

We are living in a constant state of rush. From the moment our feet hit the floor, the rush began. Never-ending until our head hits the pillow at night. But there is a better life for us. It only comes about when we place all of our faith in Jesus Christ. Humans try to do things by themselves, boastfully saying I did this, and I did that by myself. The main figure, who is God, is not honored. Together, let us put God first.

Let us pray.

Father,

Help us to always keep our eyes on You. Mankind is

tricked into believing that money and material things are more important than God. So we give respect to other things than You. Help us to be like a tree planted on solid rock, so when the wind and storms of life come, we can withstand them. We know for sure that one day, You are going to return to Earth to be our judge. What a day of rejoicing that will be. Lord, send Your Pentecost fire upon us all in Jesus' name. Don't matter what the day holds; we will withstand in Jesus' name. Thank You, Jesus, that each day You renew our strength and bring us joy. We are no longer fearful of tomorrow, knowing You are with us. Keep our eyes only on You and the things of our heavenly kingdom so that we hear well done someday. Jesus, keep us like You kept Paul, not dwelling on life's circumstances but the great day of expectation to be with You. Today, we place everything we possess in Your hands as we keep our eyes on You in Jesus' name, amen. Shalom!

____

____

____

____

____

____

179

Newness in Christ Jesus

"Therefore, if anyone is in Christ, he is a new creation. The old has passed away; behold, the new has come" (2 Corinthians 5:17, ESV). As believers, God doesn't want us to walk around carrying ancient, unnecessary baggage. Forgetting that Jesus Christ already paid the price. As "born again" Christians, God has already transformed our hearts. We must allow the Holy Spirit to guide us on the path of truth. Today, if you are feeling heavy, listless, or lost, give it to Jesus. I encourage you right now to put your burdens down and keep your eyes on Jesus Christ. This is good news for a new day.

Let us pray.

Heavenly Father,

Thank You for the joy that You brought Paul in the past, and You will do the same for us. We take nothing for granted and continue to praise and worship You in Spirit and in truth. We pray for continued blessings in Jesus' name, amen. Shalom!

Write your burdens down on the lines below and ask God to leave them here.

180

New day, caregivers!

Joy comes with the morning.

> I will exalt you, Lord,
> for you lifted me out of the depths
> and did not let my enemies gloat over me.
> Lord my God, I called to you for help,
> and you healed me.

Psalm 30:1–2 (NIV)

Caregivers, yesterday is gone; today is a new day to rejoice and be glad. For each day we are alive is another opportunity to give God praise. Let us do like King Daniel and pour out our thanksgiving to our Lord.

Let us pray.

Jesus, all praise be to You, God, for Your continued love.

Lord, right now, I choose to praise You for Your goodness and mercy. You know all our circumstances, and we don't have to feel condemnation and shame. You are always guiding and protecting us when we are in need.

God, bless us with more wisdom so that we receive the spirit of discerning what's right and wrong in Your sight. Help us, Father, to be better in our jobs, marriage, parent-

ing, home, and all the areas of our lives that need strengthening in Jesus' name. As we continue to walk in Your footsteps, Lord, be our guide and shield in Jesus' name, amen. Shalom!

____

____

____

____

____

____

181

It is rewarding to wait on God

"Wait on the Lord: be of good courage, and he shall strengthen thine heart: wait, I say, on the Lord" (Psalm 27:14, KJV). You may feel discouraged and lonely at times, or even miserable and depressed, or feel like giving up. I am here to tell you that you are not alone. The Bible says, "You will keep in perfect peace those whose minds are steadfast, because they trust in you" (Isaiah 26:3, NIV).

My encouragement to you today is that you have a friend in Jesus Christ.

"No longer do I call you servants, for the servant does not know what his master is doing; but I have called you friends, for all that I have heard from my Father I have made known to you" (John 15:15, ESV). Jesus Christ is your friend, your savior, redeemer, protector, counselor, healer, provider, and much more.

Think and speak positively, knowing that your joy and peace come from God. Sometimes we want a miracle instantly; if it is delayed, we want to throw in the towel. But there is a blessing behind every delay. Why? Because your time may not be God's time. James 1:17 (NIV) tells us, "Every good and perfect gift is from above, coming down from the Father of the heavenly lights, who does not change like shifting shadows." In times like these, allow God to keep you in His safe sanctuary. Never forget that God loves you, and Jesus Christ is Lord over all. Shalom!

____

____

____

____

____

____

182

Strength in Jesus Christ

"For God has not given us a spirit of fear, but of power and of love and of a sound mind" (2 Timothy 1:7, NKJV). There are so many things happening in the world today that cause constant visitation of fear. It would be nice to live in a world without fear. As believers, you must be prepared for that moment when fear tries to raise its head up. Boldly kick fear back to where it belongs with the Word of God.

I think back to the time when I was learning to drive a car. Fear showed up on the day I had my road test, and I failed. But I did not allow fear to win; I quickly rescheduled and passed, amen. Just think how many times in your life fear has tried or stopped you from fulfilling your dreams. By having faith in Jesus Christ, you can do all things. God loves you *so* much that He would do it all for you.

Make it a point of duty to keep the name of Jesus always on your lips and written in your heart; there is power in that name, amen. Jesus came so we all could have an abundance of life. Receive it right now in the mighty name of the True Living God, Jesus Christ. Amen. Shalom!

183

Honoring God

> Shadrach, Meshach, and Abednego, answered and said to the king, O Nebuchadnezzar, we are not careful to answer thee in this matter.
> If it be so, our God whom we serve is able to deliver us from the burning fiery furnace, and he will deliver us out of thine hand, O king.
> But if not, be it known unto thee, O king, that we will not serve thy gods, nor worship the golden image which thou hast set up.

Daniel 3:16–18 (KJV)

When you honor God, God stands up in your defense. The three men had no doubt in their hearts that God would deliver them in their time of distress. They stood up to King Nebuchadnezzar regardless of their punishment. Don't be disappointed and discouraged when things don't go the way you want them to go. You are being prepared for something greater and bigger.

Don't be afraid to go after your dreams; God will see you through. As Christians, it is alright to have a positive attitude moving forward in life. Anchor yourself in the Word of the Lord, believing in your heart you can do all things through Christ who strengthens you. Today, go after your goals in Jesus' name, amen. Shalom!

184

Love by example

> When he had washed his feet and put on his outer garments and resumed his place, he said to them, "Do you understand what I have done to you? You call me teacher and Lord, and you are right, for so I am. If I then, your Lord and Teacher, have washed your feet, you also ought to wash one another's feet. For I have given you an example, that you also should do just as I have done to you. Truly, truly, I say to you, no servant is greater than his master, nor is a messenger greater than the one who sent him."

John 13:12–16 (ESV)

Do you know what real love is? I am not asking about mere words and no action. What I am asking you about is the godly kind of love. In the scripture above, Jesus was demonstrating that kind of love. Let me explain the scene; Jesus was about to be betrayed and eventually nailed to a cross. But yet He took the time to wash the feet of His disciples. He is the Messiah, yet He serves in love.

Are you following in Jesus' footsteps? Sometimes, we are so cold and unconcerned about others and their problems. As a Christian, take a minute today and reach out to someone you have not spoken to for a while. Tell them you love them and you are there if they ever need you. This is what the Bible says, “Therefore be imitators of God, as beloved children. And walk in love, as Christ loved us and gave himself up for us, a fragrant offering and sacrifice to God” (Ephesians 5:1–2, ESV). God’s love is real, so love thy brother as thyself. God loves you, with everlasting love, amen. Shalom!

____

____

____

____

____

____

185

Walking with God

Psalm 23:4 (NIV) says, "Even though I walk through the darkest valley, I will fear no evil, for you are with me; your rod and your staff, they comfort me." This Psalm gives comfort in so many ways. You may be in your valley at this moment, but it is not for long. You may be going through some sort of distress, but God is always there. The setbacks, disappointments, tears, brokenness, hurt, loneliness, and pain are not for long. "[…] weeping may endure for a night, but joy comes in the morning" (Psalm 30:5b, NKJV). It is a relief to know that there is someone who is looking after us, amen. Allow God to lead you safely out of your valley today. Place all your trust and faith in Jesus Christ, the One who loves and cares. Walking with God is the most important step in your life. March forward in Jesus' name, amen. Shalom!

186

You are chosen by God

"Who have been chosen according to the foreknowledge of God the Father, through the sanctifying work of the Spirit, to be obedient to Jesus Christ and sprinkled with his blood: grace and peace be yours in abundance" (1 Peter 1:2, NIV). It is no accident you woke up this morning. The greater one who lives inside of you opens your eyes to see another beautiful day, amen. You are a beautiful creature made in the image of God.

If you ask God what His desires are for you and your life, He will direct you, "[…] I am the Lord your God, who teaches you what is best for you, who directs you in the way you should go" (Isaiah 48:17, NIV). My encouragement today is that God is always there; get to know Him. As Christians, our purpose is to share God's Word. If you never make Jesus Christ Lord of your life, start today. Stay in love, protected by God's grace through Jesus Christ. Have a wonderful day in Jesus' name, amen. Shalom!

____

____

____

____

____

____

187

Let God...

> May God himself, the God of peace, sanctify you through and through. May your whole spirit, soul, and body be kept blameless at the coming of our Lord Jesus Christ. The one who calls you is faithful, and he will do it.

1 Thessalonians 5:22–24 (NIV)

When we attempt to get things done without God, we mess it up; in the verses above, His instructions are very precise and clear. In order to find true peace, happiness, and joy, we must allow God to have total control.

A life without the Lord's sanctification will leave an unfulfilled void. God's Word said, "Today, if you will hear His voice: Do not harden your hearts" (Psalm 95:8, NKJV). Allow God in today, make Him Lord of your life, and receive your unlimited blessings in Jesus' name, amen. Shalom!

____

____

____

____

____

____

188

Heavenly Father

Let us pray.

Today we study Your Word in order to find Psalms that are full of hope and remind us of Your protective hand on our lives. May Your Word be a bandage of protection over our wounds. Some of Your earthly children are in pain and discomfort; some are in isolation, separated from family and friends. We pray that in the hours of induced coma and intubations, You, Lord, touch their mind. Let them live to have a testimony of Your goodness.

In moments of sorrow and loss, may Your loving embrace comfort those who are in need. Let the truth of Your Word find roots in the innermost depth of our hearts. We repeat these words in prayer over our lives in Jesus' name:

> Those who live in the shelter of the Most High will find rest in the shadow of the Almighty. This I declare about the LORD: He alone is my refuge, my place of safety; He is my God, and I trust him. For he will rescue you from every trap and protect you from deadly disease. He will cover you with his feathers. He will shelter you with his wings. His faithful promises are your armor and protection.

Psalm 91:1–4 (NLT)

Whatever we ask of You, Lord, You provide. You are ever willing and able to supply. Thank You, Lord, for Your timeliness in showing up at the right time and moment. Father, hide us today from all sickness and disease in Jesus' name. The entire world is afflicted with different viruses that are taking lives; please keep us strong in the Lord who heals.

Thank You for life itself. Thank You for the entire staff in the hospitals and nursing facilities that are unselfishly risking their lives for others. May they receive favor in Jesus' name. Let the verses of the Psalms we repeat daily to stay in our hearts and nourish our souls

In Jesus' name, amen. Shalom! What Psalm is encouraging you today?

Psalm ________.

189

A new day

"Create in me a clean heart, O God, and renew a right spirit within me" (Psalm 51:10, KJV). This morning, let us give thanks unto God for another day in the land of the living. Let us pray.

Heavenly Father,

Thank You for everything. You woke us all up for a reason. All honor and glory belong to You, Jesus. May we walk daily in the truth of Your righteousness and grace. Keep us humble and kind with love for each other in Jesus' name. Amen.

Have a productive, prosperous day in Jesus' mighty name, amen. Shalom!

____

____

____

____

____

____

190

Thankfulness

Caregivers!

> I thank my God every time I remember you. In all my prayers for all of you, I always pray with joy because of your partnership in the gospel from the first day until now, being confident of this, that he who began a good work in you will carry it on to completion until the day of Christ Jesus.
> It is right for me to feel this way about all of you, since I have you in my heart and, whether I am in chains or defending and confirming the gospel, all of you share in God's grace with me. God can testify how I long for all of you with the affection of Christ Jesus.
> And this is my prayer: that your love may abound more and more in knowledge and depth of insight, so that you may be able to discern what is best and may be pure and blameless for the day of Christ, filled with the fruit of righteousness that comes through Jesus Christ—to the glory and praise of God.

Philippians 1:3–9 (NIV)

Ever feel happy and cannot figure out why? As Christians, choosing God brings an unexplainable joy. When the trials of life come, we will overcome them and be happy in them. Never allow anyone to steal your joy, amen. In the scripture above, Paul was writing to the Phillipi people whilst he was in prison. He was encouraging them to keep the faith, love, and togetherness as one body of Christ. He was not sad; as a matter of fact, he was joyful and willing to die for what he believed in. We, as Christians, have to live the same way. In the midst of oppression and persecution, keep on smiling, singing, and praising God. My encouragement today is to let your light shine; God has the final say. Stay together in love and harmony in Jesus' name, amen. Shalom!

____

____

____

____

____

____

191

Ever-present God

"And God said, 'Let there be lights in the vault of the sky to separate the day from the night, and let them serve as signs to mark sacred times, and days and years, and let them be lights in the vault of the sky to give light on the earth.' And it was so" (Genesis 1:14–15, NIV). Our God is not only God to some people and not to others. He is God to everyone who seeks Him.

Just as He created the day and night for a purpose, it is so for us. Each one is special to God and has a purpose on this Earth. God's plan for our salvation is to have hope for a brighter tomorrow. We may be in a season of darkness, but the dawning of brighter will soon come. My encouragement is to not be disappointed and discouraged when life's challenges approach. Face each new day with great expectations. God has a plan for each of us. Don't matter where you are in your walk with God. He is in the midst, amen. Stay strong in Jesus' love, amen. Shalom!

____

____

____

____

____

____

192

Live by example

"For God so loved the world, that he gave his only begotten Son, that whosoever believeth in him should not perish, but have everlasting life" (John 3:16, KJV). It is a wonderful feeling knowing that you are loved by a perfect God. You were created out of love. God's agape love is everlasting, perfect, and unconditional, amen. Even when you fail, He keeps on loving you because God is Love.

> Love is patient, love is kind. It does not envy, it does not boast, it is not proud. It does not dishonor others, it is not self-seeking, it is not easily angered, it keeps no record of wrongs. Love does not delight in evil but rejoices with the truth. It always protects, always trusts, always hopes, always perseveres. Love never fails. But where there are prophecies, they will cease; where there are tongues, they will be stilled; where there is knowledge, it will pass away.
>
> 1 Corinthians 13:4–8 (NIV)

Throughout the Bible, you can read about the love of God for mankind. My encouragement today is to let us love one another as God loves us. You are special, have worth and value, believe and receive it, in Jesus' name, amen. Shalom!

193

Never give up

> But you, keep your head in all situations, endure hardship, do the work of an evangelist, discharge all the duties of your ministry.
> For I am already being poured out like a drink offering, and the time for my departure is near. I have fought the good fight, I have finished the race, I have kept the faith. Now there is in store for me the crown of righteousness, which the Lord, the righteous Judge, will award to me on that day—and not only to me, but also to all who have longed for his appearing.

2 Timothy 4: 5–8 (NIV)

I tell myself each day that it doesn't matter what comes my way; I will keep on praising God. I am living this life like Paul, preaching and teaching the Gospel of Christ Jesus, amen. My encouragement today is, don't matter what comes your way, hold on to Jesus. Whatever life throws at you, tell yourself, I can do all things through Christ who strengthens you, amen.

In the scripture above, Paul was writing to Timothy a letter of encouragement while he himself was in prison about to be put to death. As disciples, it is very important that you share the gospel of Christ Jesus. The Bible stated, "Study to shew thyself approved unto God, a workman that needeth not to be ashamed, rightly dividing the word of truth" (2 Timothy 2:15, KJV). As a body of believers, be strong in the Lord. Have a wonderful day in Jesus' name, amen. Shalom!

____

____

____

____

____

____

194

Thankful

"Give thanks to the LORD, for he is good; For his mercies endures forever" (Psalm 118:1, NIV).

It is a beautiful day to be alive.

Let us pray.

Almighty God,

King of kings, we praise You. We praise You for Your power and Your glory. This day, Lord, deliver us all from evil. Our hope is in Your coming to deliver us from all suffering and pain. We honor You, God, with everything You have provided unto us and more in Jesus' name. Amen.

Have a wonderful and Blessed day in Jesus' name, amen. Shalom!

____

____

____

____

____

____

195

Christian unity

How wonderful, how beautiful,
when brothers and sisters get along!
It's like costly anointing oil
flowing down head and beard,
Flowing down Aaron's beard,
flowing down the collar of his priestly robes.
It's like the dew on Mount Hermon
flowing down the slopes of Zion.
Yes, that's where God commands the blessing,
ordains eternal life.

Psalm 133:1–3 (MSG)

Caregivers, God wants us all to live in love and unity. When we live the way God desires, our eternal blessings are guaranteed.

No ill-speaking, slandering, gossiping, hate, malice. You may therefore ask why it takes place in the first place. There could be many reasons, for example, jealousy, envy, or even strife, with the main objective to cause confusion and chaos. There are enemies amongst us whose sole purpose is to distract us from God's work, amen. My advice today is to be wise and educate yourself with the Word of God. So when the enemy shows up, you can knock them back to the pit of hell. Constant prayers for the spirit of discernment are necessary.

Let us pray.

Heavenly Father,

Thank You for Your Word. Thank You for Your wisdom. Thank You, Lord, for each other. Grant us love and unity. Set our minds on things above, Lord God, and not on earthly things. Strengthen us to put into practice whatever we have received or heard or seen in You. Like little children, we seek to imitate You. May we live in peace and harmony in Jesus' name, amen. Shalom!

____

____

____

____

____

____

196

Choose God

"I will lift up mine eyes unto the hills, from whence cometh my help. My help cometh from the Lord, which made heaven and earth" (Psalm 121:1–2, KJV). Looking at what is happening in the world today, only God can fix things. I am encouraging everyone to believe together for peace in this world. Many look to social media platforms, secular blogs that do not lead to Christ, and fortune tellers for help. Does your preference matter? Oh yes, as Christians, you should choose God. Let us pray.

Dear Jesus,

Forgive me for running to the people and things of this world for help and not coming to You. Thank You for being our Helper and loving us in spite of our shortcomings. Help us remember who You are and where our help comes from. Give us strength, courage, and boldness to seek You and Your approval above all else. In Your mighty name, amen. Shalom!

____

____

____

____

____

197

Set Free

Paul wrote in Romans 8:1–4 (ESV):

> There is therefore now no condemnation for those who are in Christ Jesus. For the law of the Spirit of life has set you free in Christ Jesus from the law of sin and death. For God has done what the law, weakened by the flesh, could not do. By sending his own Son in the likeness of sinful flesh and for sin, he condemned sin in the flesh, in order that the righteous requirement of the law might be fulfilled in us, who walk not according to the flesh but according to the Spirit.

Are you carrying around guilt and shame? That inner secret that is eating you from the inside out? Today is your day to let it go; release it right now in Jesus' name. "For freedom Christ has set us free; stand firm therefore, and do not submit again to a yoke of slavery" (Galatians 5:1, ESV).

The Bible is clear that God constantly works to deliver His children from the yoke of slavery. Jesus in John 8:36 (NIV) states, "So, if the Son sets you free, you will be free indeed." Follow the guidance of the Holy Spirit today as he directs you away from sin. The enemy is driven to draw you back into the sin to entangle you, but "[…] greater is he who is in you than he that is in the world" (1 John 4:4, KJV).

The victory is already yours. Jesus has won your freedom. The battle now is for your mind. Maintain victory over that area through the power of God's Word, and the sin that seemed to be habitual will no longer have a hold over you. Live free today, for God loves you. You are no longer a slave to fear by the blood of Jesus Christ, amen. Shalom!

____

____

____

____

____

____

198

Worship God in praise

"I will praise God's name in song and glorify him with thanksgiving" (Psalm 69:30, NIV). The psalmist David reminds us how important it is to give God our best praise, along with our gratitude. David demonstrates a valuable truth through his example of praising the Lord's thanksgiving. Even in the most difficult times when you are surrounded by discouragement, praise and thanksgiving together will make a difference. They can transform your hearts, amen.

Let us pray.

Dear Heavenly Father,

I worship You because You are God. You are Lord above all others and are worthy of my daily prayers. When I am down and out, You pick me up; thank You for being faithful toward me. Your presence I yearn for every second of every day. Keep my feet on the right path to salvation. You are a good and loving Father who never leaves or forsakes me. Thank You for the sacrifice of Your Son, Jesus Christ, and now we have victory in You one day. Bless and keep us all, in Jesus' name, I pray, amen. Shalom!

199

Caregiver's prayer

"Do nothing from selfish ambition or conceit, but in humility count others more significant than yourselves. Let each of you look not only to his own interests but also to the interests of others" (Philippians 2:3–4, ESV). Most caregivers are women. Women reproduce, we lead, we care for others and nurture, and the roles women play are endless. Women give of themselves above and beyond expectations. May God continue to bless and keep all the women in this world.

Let us pray:

Lord,

As this new day begins, no one knows how it will end but You. Help us to recognize the great women who give of themselves selflessly. Many of whom are in bondage in one way or the other. We pray today for women's freedom in Jesus' name. God, You set the example by creating the first woman, Eve, from whom women were derived. Today, as we celebrate women, I pray that You touch them from the crown of their heads to the sole of their feet in Jesus' name. The women who need strengthening, do it today, Lord; where it is hurt, suffering, and pain, remove it and replace them with joy, peace, and happiness in Jesus' love. We pray all these requests in the name of Jesus, amen. Shalom!

____

____

____

____

____

____

____

200

Give Tthanks to God

> I will give you thanks, for you answered me; you have become my salvation. The stone the builders rejected has become the cornerstone; the LORD has done this, and it is marvelous in our eyes. The LORD has done it this very day; let us rejoice today and be glad. LORD, save us! LORD, grant us success! Blessed is he who comes in the name of the LORD. From the house of the LORD we bless you. The LORD is God, and he has made his light shine on us….

Psalm 118:21–27 (NIV)

As the Psalm so rightfully says, we are to give thanks at all times. In the good times, in the not-so-good times, give thanks. Whatever may be going on in your life today, continue giving thanks to God. Always remember, "Weeping may endure for a night, But joy comes in the morning" (Psalm 30:5, NKJV).

Let us pray.

Dear Heavenly Father,

Thank You for Your goodness and mercy. You have granted me another day to give You praise and honor. I will live for You, Lord, all the days of my life. In Jesus' name, amen. Shalom!

201

Unconditional love

> But Ruth replied, "Don't urge me to leave you or to turn back from you. Where you go I will go, and where you stay I will stay. Your people will be my people and your God my God. Where you die I will die, and there I will be buried. May the Lord deal with me, be it ever so severely, if even death separates you and me." When Naomi realized that Ruth was determined to go with her, she stopped urging her.
>
> Ruth 1:16–18 (NIV)

In a nutshell, the story of Naomi, Ruth, and Boaz, the three main characters, show wisdom, courage, love, and true happiness. Today, let us be determined like Ruth and love the Lord thy God with all our hearts, never turning back.

Let us pray.

Lord God,

As we meditate on Your goodness, how can we fail to extend kindness to others who are in need? Bless us with Your supernatural love and compassion toward everyone we encounter. Allow others to see Your blessings through us so that we, too, may enjoy Your beauty. May we always be kind in words and actions to others. Like Boaz, Lord, may today's men be honorable and kind to the Ruth's in their life in Jesus' name. May we always share God's love with one another in Jesus' name, amen. Shalom!

____

____

____

____

____

____

____

202

Friend of God

A friendship with God involves talking to Him and listening to Him. Do you spend quality time studying and obeying the Word of God? Hearing from God takes meditating on His Word day and night. The prophet Jeremiah 15:16 (NIV) said, "When your words came, I ate them; they were my joy and my heart's delight…." The triunity of God, Father, Son, and Holy Spirit, have your best interest at heart, amen.

Obedience is the key; Scripture instructs us: "Do not merely listen to the Word, and so deceive yourselves. Do what it says" (James 1:22, NIV). Every friend of God wants to do His will in order to please Him. "Jesus said, 'I am the way and the truth and the life. No one comes to the Father except through me. If you really knew me, you would know my Father as well…'" (John 14:6–7, NIV) In other words, there is no friendship with God without a relationship with Jesus Christ.

Those who know Jesus know the Father and the Holy Spirit as well. It is never too late to have a relationship with God; today is your day, amen. Have a wonderful weekend with your family and friends. Always remember God loves you more, amen. Shalom!

203

Be humble

> When he noticed how the guests picked the places of honor at the table, he told them this parable: "When someone invites you to a wedding feast, do not take the place of honor, for a person more distinguished than you may have been invited. If so, the host who invited both of you will come and say to you, 'Give this person your seat.' Then, humiliated, you will have to take the least important place. But when you are invited, take the lowest place, so that when your host comes, he will say to you, 'Friend, move up to a better place.' Then you will be honored in the presence of all the other guests. For all those who exalt themselves will be humbled, and those who humble themselves will be exalted."
>
> Luke 14:7–11 (NIV)

How many of us can relate to this parable? For example, presently, you might be overworked and overlooked at your job or even at your church. You may be doing above and beyond day after day, week after week, year after year without recognition. But don't worry, with a willing and cheerful heart, keep on working hard.

Someone *is* observing and recording; amen, your reward is certain. When you put yourself last, you will be promoted to first place. There are those who try to impress others conveniently, but in the end, they are seen for who they really are in the end. In the parable above, Jesus was teaching about humility.

The good work, a man, does never goes unpaid, amen. Caregivers, my encouragement today is to stay humble; your blessings are limitless. The Scripture says, "Blessed are the meek, for they will inherit the earth" (Matthew 5:5, NIV).

Let us pray.

Lord Jesus,

May we always be humble in our daily walk with You. Let us never murmur and complain, even when things are rough. You taught us by example what humility is all about; keep us focused on Jesus, amen. Shalom!

204

New Day in Christ Jesus

"O give thanks unto the Lord; for he is good: because his mercy endureth for ever" (Psalm 118:1, KJV). How beautiful it is to see another day. It is no accident or chance we are here. There is a reason why God looks after all of us, because of *love*. To God be the glory; let us pray.

Dear Heavenly Father,

Thank You for Your goodness and mercy. You give us the best of You, Lord. Help us never take it for granted and honor You with our praise and worship.

Keep us steadfast in our walk with You, Jesus, and anoint us with Your Holy Spirit. Bless and keep our friends and family in Jesus' name, amen. Shalom!

____

____

____

____

____

____

____

205

God our Comforter

When dark days come, we face the swollen river and look over to the other side. Many find comfort in these words:

> Let not your heart be troubled: ye believe in God, also believe in me. In my Father's house, there are many mansions […]. I go to prepare a place for you. And if I go and prepare a place for you, I will come again, and receive you unto myself; that where I am, there ye may be also.
>
> John 14:1–3 (KJV)

Today we remember our dear friends, relatives, and co-workers.

We stand together to celebrate their lives on this Earth. May our hearts be comforted knowing they have died in the Lord. One day we are going to be reunited again. We commit ourselves to the love and the grace of God. The Bible brings comfort and assurance of salvation to our souls. Let us keep on running this good race of life so that one day we are going to hear these words: "well done," amen. Be strong in Jesus' name, amen. Shalom!

____

____

____

____

206

Running away

So after Abram had been living in Canaan ten years, Sarai his wife, took her Egyptian slave Hagar and gave her to her husband to be his wife. He slept with Hagar, and she conceived.

When she knew she was pregnant, she began to despise her mistress. Then Sarai said to Abram, “You are responsible for the wrong I am suffering. I put my slave in your arms, and now that she knows she is pregnant, she despises me. May the Lord judge between you and me.”

“Your slave is in your hands,” Abram said. “Do with her whatever you think is best.”

Then Sarai mistreated Hagar, so she fled from her.

The angel of the Lord found Hagar near a spring in the desert; it was the spring that is beside the road to Shur. And he said, “Hagar, slave of Sarai, where have you come from, and where are you going?”

“I’m running away from my mistress Sarai,” she answered.

Then the angel of the Lord told her, “Go back to your mistress and submit to her.” The angel added, “I will increase your descendants so much that they will be too numerous to count.”

Genesis 16:3–10 (NIV)

What are you running from today? Is it unemployment? Or fear? Or a rough patch in your marriage? Poverty, addiction? Whatever it is, now is the time to stop.

Sometimes the pressures of life are overbearing, and it feels easier to just run away and hide. But that's not the solution, amen. Stand your ground; yes, stand strong in the Lord. In the scripture above, yes, there was deception. But the end result was that *all* of Abraham's descendants were blessed upon the Earth. Don't matter what you are facing today; instead of running away from circumstances, run to God. He is waiting with arms wide open to welcome you. Tremendous blessings and breakthroughs are coming your way in Jesus' name, amen. Shalom!

____

____

____

____

____

____

____

207

Caregivers, be strong!

To truly persevere:

> After Job had prayed for his friends, the Lord restored his fortunes and gave him twice as much as he had before. All his brothers and sisters and everyone who had known him before came and ate with him in his house. They comforted and consoled him over all the trouble the Lord had brought on him, and each one gave him a piece of silver and a gold ring. The Lord blessed the latter part of Job's life more than the former part…

Job 42:10–12 (NIV)

Job is the perfect example of what it means to trust in God. In life, when the challenges come, don't be too quick to throw in the towel. We have to take God at His Word; whatever He says He will do, He always does, amen.

Job had lost almost everything, even got terribly sick, but he never cursed God. Because of his strong belief in God's Word, restoration took place. You may be at that point in your life where nothing is going right. But keep on seeking and praising God; a new day of restoration is coming your way in Jesus' name.

Let us pray.

Dear Lord,

Thank You for another day; we may complain at times, but please forgive us. Give us the strength to keep holding on when it seems like it's over. Jesus, we know You have a much better plan in store for us; teach us how to depend on You and You alone. We make plans, Lord, but Your plan is better. Open the floodgates of heaven and pour out Your blessings upon us in Jesus' name, amen. Shalom!

____

____

____

____

____

____

____

208

Finding your peace in God

> So after he had washed their feet, and had taken his garments, and was set down again, he said unto them, Know ye what I have done to you?
> Ye call me Master and Lord: and ye say well; for so I am.
> If I then, your Lord and Master, have washed your feet; ye also ought to wash one another's feet.
> For I have given you an example, that ye should do as I have done to you.

John 13:12–15 (KJV)

Today, let us examine our hearts. Reminiscent of the sacrifice that was made for us all. Ask yourself, "Am I a good servant?"

We should be selfless rather than selfish, amen. Jesus' time on Earth was spent teaching by example. As disciples, let us be good examples and love one another. Reach out to that someone, ask them how things are, and also encourage them in the things of God. Our task was made easier after Jesus's resurrection. He paid the price for all of our sins at the cross. To God be the glory; if it was not for the goodness of God our Heavenly Father, where would we be? Caregivers, let us spread the love of Jesus and *love* one another, amen. May these words bring peace in your hearts in Jesus' name, amen. Shalom!

____

____

____

____

____

____

____

209

Face to face with God

It was Wednesday morning, February 9th, 2022. I was lying on my bed, just finishing my morning prayer. I turned to my left, which was almost to the edge of the bed. I felt a warm feeling or presence come over me; then, I was looked up into the brightest glowing light I had ever seen. I was looking into God's face. I felt like I was one with Him. I did not say anything because I felt nothing needed to be said. Jesus was looking down at me with a smile. At that moment, I experienced an unexplainable love. It was a feeling that I wanted to last forever; it did last throughout the day. I shared my experience with a few close friends, family, and my husband.

This is my actual message to my daughter that morning, "Hi Lady, hope all is well. I saw Jesus this morning and felt so happy. I was lying on the bed, looking up into His face. I am not losing my mind when I say God is real. Keep trusting God."

We spoke after, and I further explained. I had many encounters with God throughout my life, but that morning, my Father revealed Himself to me.

The reason I am sharing this morning is that someone

needs to hear that God is real. Hallelujah, hallelujah! My God lives. If God can do it for me, He can surely do it for you. Isaiah 1:18 (KJV) says, "Come now, and let us reason together, saith the Lord: though your sins be as scarlet, they shall be as white as snow; though they be red like crimson, they shall be as wool."

God loves you with His everlasting love, amen.

Let us pray.

Dear Lord,

Thank You for your goodness and mercy. Thank You for the opportunity to see another day. May Your warm embrace protect and guide us, Your children. Father, keep us from harm in Jesus' name, amen. Shalom!

____

____

____

____

____

____

____

210

Don't underestimate God's power

> David said to the Philistine, "You come against me with sword and spear and javelin, but I come against you in the name of the Lord Almighty, the God of the armies of Israel, whom you have defied. This day the Lord will deliver you into my hands, and I'll strike you down and cut off your head. This very day I will give the carcasses of the Philistine army to the birds and the wild animals, and the whole world will know that there is a God in Israel. All those gathered here will know that it is not by sword or spear that the Lord saves; for the battle is the Lord's, and he will give all of you into our hands."
>
> 1 Samuel 17:45–47 (NIV)

Back in those days, David was looked down upon in scorn because he placed all his trust in God. His own people doubted him, and the enemies made fun of him. Read the entire book of 1 Samuel to get a better understanding.

Fast forward, small boy David went on to defeat and kill the giant that everyone was so afraid of. He did not need a sword or any of the recommended gear. All he was certain of he had was the Lord's favor upon him, and that's all that mattered. Today, many of us may be facing some form of Goliath in our lives. Let us do like David, amen.

Place all of our trust in God. Let *God* fight our battles. Don't just take what people suggest; take what God says:

> Put on the full armor of God so that you can take your stand against the devil's schemes. For our struggle is not against flesh and blood, but against the rulers, against the authorities, against the powers of this dark world, and against the spiritual forces of evil in the heavenly realms. Therefore put on the full armor of God so that when the day of evil comes, you may be able to stand your ground, and after you have done everything, to stand. Stand firm then, with the belt of truth buckled around your waist, with the breastplate of righteousness in place, and with your feet fitted with the readiness that comes from the gospel of peace. In addition to all this, take up the shield of faith, with which you can extinguish all the flaming arrows of the evil one. Take the helmet of salvation and the sword of the Spirit, which is the word of God.

Ephesians 6:11–17 (NIV)

Allow God to fight for you. Have a wonderful day in Jesus' name, amen. Shalom!

____

____

____

____

____

211

No longer slaves to fear

"For freedom, Christ has set us free; stand firm therefore, and do not submit again to a yoke of slavery" (Galatians 5:1, ESV). Let us give thanks to God for His mercies and grace towards us. Let us pray.

Heavenly Father,

Today, thank You for sustaining our country. This country, Lord, was built on strong biblical values. That is why we, Your people, have the freedom to worship You publicly. Other countries do not have such privileges. We are free to pray. We are free to read Your Word. We are free to preach and share the Word of Jesus Christ. For this, we are forever grateful.

Today, we also pray for our Christian brothers and sisters who are being persecuted or even killed because of their faith. Keep us aware of those who are against us and would stop at nothing to destroy the Christian doctrine. Lord, grant our leaders and those in authority the wisdom to abide by the godly principles of our ancestors. Help us to stand strong in You and for Your purposes.

Thank You for Your everlasting presence; thank You for Your truth that says, "Who the Son sets free is free," indeed! True freedom is only found in Jesus Christ alone; keep our eye on You, amen. Shalom!

212

I am proud to be me

> For you created my inmost being;
> you knit me together in my mother's womb.
> I praise you because I am fearfully and wonderfully made;
> your works are wonderful,
> I know that fully well…
>
> Psalm 139:13–14 (NIV)

God does not make mistakes, amen.

We are living in a world where so many people feel insecure and unsure of themselves. Billboards, advertisements, television, and all social media help to make us feel inadequate. But today, I want to let you know that the living God we serve doesn't care whether we are fat or thin, tall or short, light skin or dark skin, amen. We were all made beautiful in God's image; use your God-given authority to stand tall and strong in the Lord.

"Behold, I give unto you power to tread on serpents and scorpions, and over all the power of the enemy: and nothing shall by any means hurt you" (Luke 10:19, KJV). I am telling you! Yes, you! be proud of who you are. Have a wonderful day, in Jesus' name, amen. Shalom!

213

God cares

Good morning, caregivers!

Psalm 23 (KJV) is one of the Psalms I first learned as a youth. It always brings great comfort knowing that someone is looking after me and guiding my steps. Today, I want to encourage all who are reading to really think about each word deeply, amen.

Let us read together:

> The LORD is my shepherd; I shall not want.
> He maketh me lie down in green pastures: he leadeth me beside the still waters.
> He restoreth my soul: he leadeth me in the paths of righteousness for his name's sake.
> Yea, though I walk through the valley of the shadow of death, I will fear no evil: for thou art with me; thy rod and thy staff they comfort me.
> Thou preparest a table before me in the presence of mine enemies: thou anointest my head with oil; my cup runneth over.
> Surely goodness and mercy shall follow me all the days of my life: and I will dwell in the house of the LORD for ever.

How do you feel after reading this Psalm? Personally, I am screaming, "Thank You, Jesus! Hallelujah!" As a matter of fact, I know that our Father in heaven loves us no matter what, amen. Come, let's fellowship together with the plans God has for us all. Have a wonderful day in Jesus' name, amen. Shalom!

____

____

____

____

____

____

____

214

God's will

Good morning!

God has a plan for each and every one of us. It is to prosper and reap the benefits of the Earth. And remember, it's not for some only; it's for everyone, amen. Proverbs 16:9 (NKJV) explains, "A man's heart plans his way, But the LORD directs his step." Ever got saved from something really bad? Later, looking back, you can say if it was not for God's grace and mercy, I would not be alive or even here! It is God's plan to protect and look after us.

The trees, birds, animals, and more, God created and looked after them. Whatever your plan is, take it to God first and ask Him to reveal His plan for your life. If you wait a bit, you will surely hear from Him, amen. Keep your eyes on Jesus today and allow Him to lead you His way. Have a great day in Jesus' name, amen. Shalom!

____

____

____

____

____

____

____

215

Faith in God changes everything

Hebrews 11:6 (NIV) so rightly says, "But without faith it is impossible to please him: for he that cometh to God must believe that he is, and that he is a rewarder of them that diligently seek him." It relieves all the pressure on this human body, knowing that Jesus is carrying all of our burdens and pain. I believe what Jesus said, and therefore I am healed, I am strong, I am rich, I have been delivered, and it is finished.

When we rely on Jesus Christ, we can rest, believing that everything is already done, amen. Speak positive words over yourself, your family, your friends, and even your enemies, amen. "The tongue has the power of life and death, and those who love it will eat its fruit" (Proverbs 18:21, NIV). When we speak positive words, we will receive positive results if we speak the opposite, the results will be negative. Trusting in God will always lift us up, amen. We are responsible for our words. So, let's practice repeating faith-filled words because it's already done in Jesus Christ, amen. Shalom!

____

____

216

God first

As this great commandment says, "You shall love the Lord your God with all your heart and with all your soul and with all your mind" (Matthew 22:37, ESV). It does not hurt to remind ourselves daily that God is good. As a matter of fact, we make lists of what to do regularly. How often is God part of the to-do list? Starting from today, let's put God first on our to-do list, amen. When we put God first, He will always put us first in His kingdom. Have a wonderful day with your family and friends in Jesus' name, amen. Shalom!

217

I say yes!

“But seek ye first the kingdom of God, and his righteousness; and all these things shall be added unto you” (Matthew 6:33, KJV). Do you say yes to Jesus Christ today? If Jesus was to show up this very minute, would you be ready for Him? If you will not, don’t wait another second. Stop what you are doing!

Ask God to come into your life, change you from the inside out, and forgive you for all your sins. Let Him know from this moment onwards that you will live for Him all the days of your life in Jesus’ name, amen. By making Jesus Christ the Lord of your life, you are a new person in Christ, amen. At the speed of this life we are living, tomorrow may be too late.

Now, as Christians, let’s not play around and get serious about the things of God. Some are called to be leaders; some are teachers; some are prophets/prophetess, evangelists, apostles, or disciples in one capacity or another we were called to serve. It is your time to live in the overflow of God’s richest blessings, amen. Have a wonderful, beautiful day with your family and friends in Jesus’ name, amen. Shalom!

218

Jesus our Comforter

In such a time of senseless killings, crimes, wars, and hate, this world needs a Comforter. He is the only one: Jesus Christ of Nazareth. Today, let us pray for all the chaos that is happening. This is where we, as Christians, come in! We are to stand in the gap for others, amen.

Let us pray.

Dear Heavenly Father,

When we cry out to You, You hear our voices, and we are so thankful that we can seek You through prayer, anytime and anywhere. Today, we bring the blood of innocent people before You because only You are able to stop it. Your promises are to protect those in need and bring justice where needed.

May Your Spirit intercede in the heart of mankind and stir up love for each other instead of hate. Today, touch the hearts of those in authority that they will seek You first in every decision that they make in Jesus' name.

Thank You for the deep relationship we can have with You through prayer.

Today, Lord, we agree in prayer because Your prom-

ises are always "yes" and "amen." Father, as we pray for the people of this world, we know only You hold the solution to all the confusion. Jesus, You healed the broken-hearted and are our comforter in times of sorrow. Today, we place everything in Your hands in Jesus' mighty name, amen. Shalom!

____

____

____

____

____

____

____

219

God is always with us

Caregivers, let us read this Psalm together.

> I will praise you, O LORD, with all my heart; before the "gods" I will sing your praise.
> I will bow down toward your holy temple and will praise your name for your love and your faithfulness, for you have exalted above all things your name and your word.
> When I called, you answered me; you made me bold and stouthearted.
> May all the kings of the earth praise you, O LORD, when they hear the words of your mouth.
> May they sing of the ways of the LORD, for the glory of the LORD is great.
> Though the LORD is on high, he looks upon the lowly, but the proud he knows from afar.
> Though I walk in the midst of trouble, you preserve my life; you stretch out your hand against the anger of my foes, with your right hand you save me.
> The LORD will fulfill [His purpose] for me; your love, O LORD, endures forever—do not abandon the works of your hands.

Psalm 138 (NIV)

As God's children, we are never alone. During political turmoil, a pandemic, sickness, or loss, God has not abandoned us. Sometimes we need to be reminded that one of the final promises that Jesus made to us was, "[…]. And surely I am with you always, to the very end of the age" (Matthew 28:20b, NIV). As we maneuver our daily lives, always remember you are not alone. Have a wonderful day in Jesus' name, amen. Shalom!

___

___

___

___

___

___

___

220

New day

> Therefore if any man be in Christ, he is a new creature: old things have passed away; behold, all things have become new. Now all things are of God, who has reconciled us to himself through Jesus Christ, and has given us the ministry of reconciliation, that is, that God was in Christ reconciling the world to himself, not imputing their trespasses to them, and has committed to us the word of reconciliation.
> Now then, we are ambassadors for Christ, as though God were pleading through us: we implore you on Christ's behalf, be reconciled to God. For he made him who knew no sin to be sin for us, that we might become the righteousness of God in him.

2 Corinthians 5:17–20 (KJV)

Are you walking in the footsteps of God? Are you representing what God represents? What is holding you back from going all out for the kingdom of God? Whatever it may be that is holding you back, rest it down, and equip yourself with the full armor of Christ. Our earthly mandate as Christians is to be ambassadors for Christ and the kingdom of heaven, amen. God sent His only Son, Christ Jesus, to die so we can be set free from all of our sins.

That is the reconciliation that has been referred to in this scripture. The good news is that all our sins have been washed away, making us believers brand new. No more worrying about the past and what you may have done. This is the best feeling ever, hallelujah. You, yes, you are free! Free from condemnation, free from guilt, free from shame, and free from mental pain. This is the moment when you ought to shout out loud: "Thank You, Lord; thank You, Jesus, for reconciling me in Jesus' name! Amen. Shalom!"

___

___

___

___

___

___

___

221

Share God's love

The scripture says, "For God so loved the world, that he hath given his only begotten Son, that whosoever believeth in him, should not perish, but have everlasting life" (John 3:16, KJV).

Many in this crowded world may feel lonely because they have lost touch with the inner love of Christ. But God is Love; He wants to fill your hearts till it overflows, amen. In all the turmoil, many small things may pass by unnoticed. Do we want to stand alone, or do we want to reach out and meet that someone halfway?

This world is full of beauty that people do not see. Many run around hectic going from here to there to earn their living and to earn a lot of worldly treasures. They forget there are things that are much more worthwhile than all the money they would be able to gather in their life.

How much do we want to open our arms to those we do not know and those we might know? My prayers today are for us to be our brother's keeper. Don't just talk love but show love by example, amen. Let us begin the work week right by sharing God's love.

Stay blessed in Jesus' name, amen. Shalom!

222

Our big God

When we pray, remember you are worshiping the Only, Big, True Living God, who holds the entire world in His hands, amen. To all women, with or without children, you are honored each and every day of your lives by God's grace.

Let's pray.

Dear Jesus,

Majestic King, we honor You. We acknowledge that You rule the universe with love. Thank You for creating us in Your image and likeness. Continue to guide and protect us in everything that we do. You are "El Shaddai, "the "All-Sufficient One," the God who is more than enough. We place our hands in Yours, with faith in Jesus' name, amen. Shalom!

____

____

____

____

____

____

____

223

Take a moment to pray

"Let us then approach God's throne of grace with confidence, so that we may receive mercy and find grace to help us in our time of need" (Hebrews 4:16, KJV). Don't let sin keep you from praying. If you haven't prayed today or in a while, take five minutes today and close your eyes—thank God for who He is and who He has made you be. Ask Him to forgive any sin in your life, especially the sin that has been holding you back from Him. Let His love pour over you and refresh you.

Let us pray.

Dear God,

We give praise because You are worthy. Many times we ignore what You are showing us and stray, but You always lead us back to You. Keep our thoughts always focused on the things of You. Even though we may get distracted from You, guide us back in Jesus' name. You are worthy of all praise. Because Your spirit dwells within us, we are heirs to Your kingdom. Thank You for the gift of eternal life with You. Thank You for Your love as we stay in Your footsteps in Jesus' name, amen. Shalom!

224

Blessed morning, caregivers!

Putting all your trust in God.

First John 4:4 (NIV) encourages us with the truth, "You, dear children, are from God and have overcome them, because the one who is in you is greater than the one who is in the world." Be prepared as Christians to do battle for Christ. We are living in a world that is changing its concepts every day. For instance, look around you at the news, and you will see the hate that is handed out to Christians. We have to be strong in the Lord, never forgetting what Jesus experienced when He walked the Earth. He was jeered at, ridiculed, called names, mocked, laughed at, spat upon, beaten, pierced, hung on a cross, and eventually killed. The good news is He arose from the grave. The same spirit that was with Jesus is living within us today. Have no fear when we suffer persecution because of our faith; God has a greater reward for us, with Him, in heavenly places.

Let us pray.

Dear God,

Thank You for Your living Word! As was clearly described as "God-breathed..." (2 Timothy 3:16, NIV). The many parables in the Bible are to set us on the perfect pathway to righteousness. God, Your love for us is amazing; help us at all times to remain constant and faithful. There is no other love that is greater than Yours! Lord, grant us the courage to step out in faith to bring forth Your Word unashamedly. As Your disciples, we asked for the right words in our mouths to meet the needs of Your people in Jesus' name. Any stumbling blocks that may be a hindrance to our discipleship are removed today in Jesus' name. Thank You for being our strength so we can depend on You. Thank You for being our Lord and Savior in Jesus' name, amen Shalom!

____

____

____

____

____

____

____

225

The healing God

Exodus 15:26b (KJV) says, "[…] for I am the LORD that healeth thee." Are you in need of healing today? There is only one solution, Jehovah Rapha—the God who heals. God wants us healthy and healed in every area of our lives. It is a commitment; just come to God. By having faith and that commitment to God, He heals us, He heals our hearts, He heals our souls, He heals our minds, and He heals our bodies. But we must come to Him in faith and experience it for ourselves. Let God lead you to that holy place of trust, rest, and salvation in Jesus Christ. Let us pray.

Dear Jesus,

Have mercy upon us. We pray this day for Your healing touch. Help us in all areas of doubt and unbelief. Grant us courage and faith to place all of our trust in You and to worry not. Abba Father, we thank You for working all things out for our good in Jesus' name, amen. Shalom!

____

____

____

____

____

____

____

226

God is our source

"And my God will meet all your needs according to his glorious riches in Christ Jesus" (Philippians 4:19, NIV). What are your needs today? Whatever it may be, God is able to supply, amen.

Let us pray.

Dear God,

We thank You that no situation is too far out of Your control to provide, for You are Jehovah-Jireh, the God who provides. We thank You that You own it all and hold everything in Your hands. We thank You that You know our needs before we even ask, before we even come to You. You're aware of all that concerns us, and You have a plan. You hold the provision; You have the solution. You alone can move mountains to make way for Your children.

We ask for Your answer, in Your timing, in Your plan, to be given for every need that weighs our hearts down. Forgive us for doubting You, worrying, and trying so hard to work everything out on our own. Help us to trust You more; help us in our unbelief. We choose to recognize and to believe that You are able to accomplish far more, to do far greater than we even thought possible. We thank You in advance for Your miracles, for paving out pathways, and for Your provision for those who love You.

Thank You for the abundance of blessings and goodness You have already stored up. We trust You this day and every day and are so grateful for Your power and joy that fills our lives. Thank You for teaching us to be content in all circumstances; we love You, Lord, and we're leaning on You in Jesus' name, amen. Shalom!

____

____

____

____

____

____

____

About the Author

Undine Brereton was born in the Caribbean island of Trinidad and Tobago. She grew up in a Christian home but strayed from the church. Undine migrated to the United States many years ago, and she faced and overcame many challenges. As an immigrant, her roots in Jesus Christ are what keep her alive. Undine is a mother of four and a friend to most who knows her. After many stumbles and fumbles in life, she found her purpose as a caregiver herself.

For many years she worked two and three jobs, where she had to wear many hats. Some of them are certified nursing assistant (CNA), baby nurse specialist, nanny/ caregiver, medical assistant (CMA), geriatric specialist, health coach, phlebotomist, and theologian in the making. Undine is happily married and is a student of Regent University. Her joy is to study and write God's inspired books only.

Closing Note

These are only a few of the hundreds of stories one can relate to as an immigrant. For those who think that they came to this country and had it easy, thank God. And those who are still hiding in the shadows, keep on trusting God for your miracle. To all caregivers, stand strong in the Lord. To the many caregivers who could not work virtually, risked their lives, and died, we salute you. May your souls rest in peace; one day, we will meet again in heaven. To God be the power and the glory.

When I migrated from Trinidad, my daughter was one of my children left behind. It was difficult for her; I always thank God for keeping and protecting her. I have included this song at the end because it was written by my daughter, Afiya Clarke (*with permission*).

"My Tears Disappeared"

Verse 1
I opened my eyes to see the most remarkably sight,
A message sent from you to me approaching in flight.
I tried to understand this thing, and then I remembered…
How could I forget, you would answer me when I called…
How could I forget, you would never see me fall.

Chorus

It came from above, in the image of a dove,

And I held it in my hand; this I knew was God's plan.

And my tears disappeared as my ears began to hear…

The word from God, the word from the Lord.

Verse 2

I think of my life before and what I went through,

So crazy and hard, you know, but the Bible stayed true.

I knelt on my knees and prayed those gray clouds just went away,

He was my friend, a person I can lean on…

He is my friend, to see me through all storms.

Chorus

It came from above, in the image of a dove,

And I held it in my hand; this I knew was God's plan.

And my tears disappeared as my ears began to hear…

The word from God, the word from the Lord.

Verse 3

Sacrifices and hell He paid, I can't dare to do,

Forget all the pain. He says I overcame that for you.

The miraculous man from God, Jesus, I can't dare to lose,

What You've done for me, no one can ever compare,

Died on Calvary, and You rose, still living here.

Chorus

It came from above, in the image of a dove,

And I held it in my hand; this I knew was God's plan.

And my tears disappeared as my ears began to hear…

The word from God, the word from the Lord.

Verse 4 (x2)

Would you give Him,

Would you give Him all you've got?

Would you be true,

Would you praise Him till you drop?

I was so lost, now I'm free, now I'm found,

I just couldn't see, but He opened my eyes for me.

Chorus

It came from above, in the image of a dove,

And I held it in my hand; this I knew was God's plan.

And my tears disappeared as my ears began to hear…

The word from God *(That's right!)*

It came from above, in the image of a dove,

And I *grasped* it in my hand; this I knew was God's plan.

And my tears disappeared as my ears began to hear…

The word from God (*The word from Jesus).*

The word from God *(Glorify Jehovah).*

The word from God *(Oh my Savior).*

The word from the Lord. *(That's right!)*

The word from God, the word…from the Lord

CPSIA information can be obtained
at www.ICGtesting.com
Printed in the USA
BVHW052057170323
660677BV00002B/3